PUBLISH, Flourish, and Make a Difference

Edited by
Festus E. Obiakor
Bob Algozzine
Fred Spooner

A GUIDE TO SUCCESSFUL WRITING IN EDUCATION

 Council for

Publish, Flourish, and Make a Difference

ISBN 0-86586-446-2

Copyright 2010 by Council for Exceptional Children, 1110 North Glebe Road, Suite 300, Arlington, Virginia 22201-5704

Stock No. P5950

Graphic Design and Layout: Carol Leigh Williams

Printed in the United States of America

10 9 8 7 6 5 4 3 2 1

Table of Contents

List of Tables and Figures

Foreword

Many aspiring writers, even those with good ideas and strong technical skills, have difficulty getting published. Without appropriate knowledge and skills, a well-developed plan for manuscript development, and a clear understanding about the publication process, many would-be authors fail. Often, they labor over papers that do not get published and research proposals that do not get funded. *Publish and Flourish: A Guide for Writing in Education* (now *Publish, Flourish, and Make a Difference: A Guide to Successful Writing in Education*) was first developed as a service to the profession to address some of the common problems novice writers face. It represented the collective knowledge and experience of many leading special education authors and editors. Although this book was designed primarily to facilitate the writing and publishing efforts of doctoral students and early-career faculty, it quickly became a valued teaching tool and reference guide used by many established scholars and educators in the field.

Over the past decade, thousands of aspiring and established writers have turned to this book to help them understand many critical dimensions of successful writing and publishing. I have used it regularly with my graduate students, and I have recommended it to colleagues on several occasions. In addition, I frequently have given copies to former students and new faculty colleagues as they enter higher education. Their testimonies on this book have been extremely positive.

As I reviewed this new edition, I was pleased to see how well the editors—Festus E. Obiakor, Bob Algozzine, and Fred Spooner—and the chapter authors have addressed many important publishing rudiments and technology changes that have occurred over the past decade, while maintaining and updating the most critical aspects of the first edition. By focusing attention on the essential knowledge, skills, and dispositions that writers need to be successful, *Publish, Flourish, and Make a Difference* addresses many day-to-day challenges all authors face (e.g., balancing competing professional responsibilities) with common sense and productive direction. As the authors tackle a broad array of topics, they provide honest and sound advice. Their thoughtful observations, sage guidance, and focused candor represent some of the best writing and thinking our field has to offer—enjoy!

Chriss Walther-Thomas, Ph.D.
University of Kansas

Preface

In our first edition of this book, we titled it, *Publish and Flourish* with the simple intention of encouraging more voices in general and special education. In this second edition, we title it, *Publish, Flourish, and Make a Difference* to challenge new and experienced scholars to continue to write in order to make a positive difference in their respective professions. We continue to believe many voices are still hidden and invisible due to challenges associated with professional writing and its intricacies. For example, in higher education, coupled with teaching loads and service activities professors are required to engage in research and other scholarly activities. Traditionally, this results in competing relationships among teaching, research, and service. We appreciate the difficulties in addressing this potentially difficult dilemma in professional discourse and development; however, we positively know (a) teachers who are great scholars and professionals, (b) scholars who are great teachers and professionals, and (c) professionals who are great teachers and scholars. Put another way, we choose to see cooperative opportunities rather than competitive relationships among the professorial imperatives of teaching, research, and service. Our experiences tell us that it is not impossible to excel in all of them.

It is common knowledge that teachers have a lot to share through writing and researchers teach a lot with their writing, especially in the growth of their professions and knowledge within their fields. Both activities contribute to and benefit from professional service. As scholars, we have excelled in teaching, research, and service. But, we continue to grow—writing has created this possibility and many other possibilities for our growth. *Publish, Flourish, and Make a Difference* is a book that resulted from years of experience engaged in and supporting professional development. We are convinced that the profession has more stories to tell and that these stories will continue to be hidden and invisible unless more of us tell them by overcoming the challenges of writing. As a consequence, we must write; and most importantly, we must take advantage of a book of this nature.

Generally, *Publish, Flourish, and Make a Difference* proactively addresses some of the "why" and "how" of telling stories in writing. To accomplish this, we invited individuals who understand the trials and tribulations of writing and frequently share their ideas. All of the chapters in this book show that writing can be challenging, but that it can also be rewarding. We believe contributing scholars of these chapters have answered many of the difficult questions about writing. It is our hope that this book presents a clear, proactive picture of the wonderful activity known as technical and professional writing. In reality, nothing is easy; writing is not an exception! But, the victory does not go to the critic who does not write—it remains with the writer who has dared to share his/her stories in writing. In the words of Theodore Roosevelt, the 26th President of the United States of America (1901–1911) during his speech in Sorbonne, France in 1910,

> It is not the critic who counts, not the man [woman] who points out how the strong man [woman] stumbled, or where the doer of deeds could have done better. The credit belongs to the man [woman] who is actually in the arena, whose face is marred by dust and sweat and blood, who strives valiantly, who errs and comes short again and again, who knows the great enthusiasms, the great devotions, and spends himself [herself] in a worthy cause, who at best knows achievement and who at the worst if he [she] fails at least fails while daring greatly so that his [her] place shall never be with those cold and timid souls who know neither victory nor defeat.

Clearly, *Publish, Flourish, and Make a Difference* is a book for new and seasoned writers. It is also a useful tool for undergraduate and graduate students. To be specific, doctoral students will find it very beneficial. Editors, mentors, scholars, researchers, and teachers can better help their students and each other by using this book in classes, presentations, and professional development. This book is for all those interested in unveiling their hidden voices through writing.

We had fun writing this book; we learned a lot during this process. We thank the Council for Exceptional Children for its interest in developing the second edition of this book.

We also want to express our gratitude to our contributing scholars and Chriss Walther-Thomas for writing the Foreword of this edition. Finally, we thank our families and colleagues for their unflinching support in this rewarding venture.

Festus E. Obiakor

Bob Algozzine

Fred Spooner

About the Contributors

Bob Algozzine, Ph.D., is a professor in the Department of Educational Leadership and Director of the Behavior and Reading Improvement Center at the University of North Carolina at Charlotte. He has published widely on issues and practical matters related to assessment and effective teaching. He has served as editor, associate editor, and field reviewer for numerous professional journals in general and special education and is currently the co-editor of *Career Development for Exceptional Individuals, Multicultural Learning and Teaching, Teacher Education and Special Education,* and *The Journal of Special Education.* He continues to take great joy from mentoring young and experienced scholars interested in sharing their writing.

Bob Audette, Ph.D., is an associate professor in the Department of Reading and Elementary Education at the University of North Carolina at Charlotte. His professional writing interests include generational poverty, effective teaching, appropriate assessment, and the use of Total Quality Education. He has served as a state-level administrator of innovative special education programs, and currently coordinates a writing group for new faculty at the university.

Jeffery P. Bakken, Ph.D., is a Professor and Chair, Department of Special Education at Illinois State University, Normal. His specific areas of interest include transition, teacher effectiveness, assessment, learning strategies, and technology. He has written more than 80 publications, including a book, journal articles, chapters, monographs, reports, and proceedings; he has made over 190 presentations at local, state, regional, national, and international levels. Additionally, he is on the editorial boards of many scholarly publications, including *Multicultural Learning and Teaching, Remedial and Special Education,* and *Multiple Voices.* Through his works, he has committed himself toward improving teachers' knowledge and techniques as well as services for students with exceptionalities and their families.

Anne Bauer, Ed.D., is a professor of special education and NCATE coordinator at the University of Cincinnati, Ohio. She is the author of 18 books and several chapters on classroom management and early childhood special education. She has served on many editorial boards including *Behavioral Disorders* and *Remedial and Special Education,* and has served as co-editor of *Teacher Education and Special Education,* the Council for Exceptional Children's teacher education division publication.

Dave L. Edyburn, Ph.D., is a professor in the Department of Exceptional Education at the University of Wisconsin-Milwaukee. He is the author of several books and numerous book chapters and journal articles on the use of technology to enhance teaching, learning, and performance. He has served as editor of *TEACHING Exceptional Children, Learning Disability Quarterly,* and *Remedial and Special Education.*

Bridgie Alexis Ford, Ph.D., is Professor and Chair, Department of Curricular and Instructional Studies at the University of Akron, Ohio. She is also Director of the Center for Urban and Higher Education in the College of Education. She is the author and co-author of several works, including two books related to the general and special education of African American learners. She served as the first editor of *Multiple Voices,* the publication of the Division for Culturally and Linguistically Diverse Exceptional Learners (DDEL), the Council for Exceptional Children. Additionally, she has served on editorial boards or as field reviewer for general and special education publications including *Multicultural Learning and Teaching,* a refereed multidisciplinary international online journal (www.mltonline.org), and *Urban Education.*

Mark B. Goor, Ph.D., is Dean of the College of Education and Organizational Leadership at the University of La Verne in southern California. He is author and co-author of several articles and chapters focusing on general and special education. He has reviewed manuscripts for many scholarly journals, including *Intervention in School and Clinic* and *Multiple Voices.*

Thierry Kolpin, Ph.D., is an assistant professor of school counseling in the College of Education and Organizational Leadership at the University of La Verne in southern California. He focuses his writings on innovative counseling and educational techniques to reach all learners.

Teresa Mehring, Ph.D., is Provost and Vice-President for Academic Affairs and Student Life and Professor of Psychology and Special Education at Emporia State University, Kansas. She has over 50 publications including books, assessment instruments, book chapters, and refereed journal articles. She is the author (in collaboration with Festus E. Obiakor and John O. Schwenn) of the 1997 book, *Disruption, Disaster, and Death: Helping Students Deal with Crises* published by the Council for Exceptional Children. She has had more than 20 grants funded by state and federal agencies and private foundations. She is on the editorial board of *Intervention in School and Clinic* and reviews for many publishing companies.

Lilia D. Monzó, Ph.D., is an assistant professor of education in the College of Educational Studies at Chapman University, Orange, California. She studies the cultural productions of Latino immigrant children and families, and the educational contexts in which they engage.

Kagendo Mutua, Ph.D., is an associate professor of special education at the University of Alabama, Tuscaloosa. Her work focuses on adolescents with severe disabilities and other marginalized groups in terms of limited access to opportunities, lack of proactive agency supports, and desired adult outcomes. She is a co-developer and co-director of Crossing Points, a model transition program serving youth with severe disabilities. She is the author and co-author of many articles and co-editor of several books, including the book series *Research on Education in Africa, Caribbean, and the Middle East.*

Festus E. Obiakor, Ph.D., is a professor in the Department of Exceptional Education at the University of Wisconsin-Milwaukee. He is an internationally known teacher-scholar, professional, and consultant with landmark works in general and special education. He has written more than 150 academic publications, including books, chapters, journal articles, and volumes of poetry. Additionally, he has served as (a) the first African American associate editor of *Exceptional Children*, the leading research journal in the field; (b) the first African American male associate editor of *Teacher Education and Special Education*, a division journal of the Council for Exceptional Children; and (c) the co-editor of *Multiple Voices*, a division journal of the Council for Exceptional Children. Currently, he is a member of the editorial boards of many scholarly referred journals. In fact, he is the co-executive editor of *Multicultural Learning and Teaching*, a refereed multidisciplinary international online journal (www.mltonline.org). He continues to mentor writers interested in unveiling their hidden "multiple" voices and talents.

James R. Patton, Ed.D., is the executive editor of PRO-ED Publishing Company, Austin, Texas, and an adjunct associate professor in the Department of Special Education at the University of Texas at Austin. In his role as Executive Editor, he is in charge of the Books and Materials Division (i.e., the acquisition and development of quality products) and negotiates contracts with potential authors. He is the author of many hooks, chapters, and articles, and he continues to serve as an editorial board member of many scholarly journals.

Stefani Roth came to CEC in 2004 and currently serves as the Director of Program Development for CEC's Professional Development Services department. In this capacity, she manages CEC's product development program which seeks to provide special educators with the tools needed to succeed in the classroom and ensure that children and youth with disabilities are academically successful. Specifically, she oversees CEC's two well-respected and often referenced professional journals, *Exceptional Children* and *TEACHING Exceptional Children*, in addition to acquisitions, product development, manuscript development, and identifying innovative delivery of content now and into the future. Before embarking on a career in publications, she served as an educator in preschool, middle school and high school settings.

Robert Rueda, Ph.D., is Professor of Psychology in Education and former Chair of the Division of Learning and Instruction at the University of Southern California. He has published widely in the areas of general and special education, psychology, and bilingualism. His current focus is on learning and motivational factors in bilingual classrooms in the areas of reading and literacy. He has served on the editorial board of several professional journals, including associate editor of the *American Educational Research Journal,* and was the first associate editor of *Exceptional Children* from a minority background.

John O. Schwenn, Ph.D., is President of Dalton State College, Georgia. He previously was Vice President for Academic Affairs and Professor of Special Education in the Division of Psychology and Special Education at Emporia State University, Kansas. He has over 40 publications and has co-authored eight books, including *More Time to Teach.* He has written and obtained grants for many innovative programs such as Project Partnership at Emporia State University. He has served on the editorial board of numerous journals, including *Multiple Voices* and *Exceptional Children.*

Fred Spooner, Ph.D., is a professor in the Department of Special Education and Child Development, University of North Carolina at Charlotte. From 1987–1996, he served as co-editor of *TEACHING Exceptional Children (TEC).* In his capacity as co-editor, he mentored writers interested in publishing works that are practitioner friendly. He has co-authored numerous books, chapters, and articles on distance learning and general and special education issues. He is currently a reviewer for many scholarly journals, an associate editor for *Research and Practice for Persons with Severe Disabilities,* and co-editor of *The Journal of Special Education.*

Martha Thurlow, Ph.D., is Director of the National Center on Educational Outcomes and Senior Research Associate, Institute on Community Interaction and Department of Educational Psychology, at the University of Minnesota.

She has published numerous books, articles, and training materials for use by professionals in general and special education and school psychology. She has served as editor, associate editor, and field reviewer for a variety of scholarly journals, including those focused on special education, assessment, and research.

Chriss Walther-Thomas, Ph.D., is Professor and Chair, Department of Special Education at the University of Kansas, Lawrence. Her scholarly works have been published in well-known journals.

Kenneth A. Weaver, Ph.D., is Interim Associate Dean and Professor of Psychology of the Teachers College of Emporia State University, Kansas. He has authored 50 articles, chapters, and books and reviews for many journals and publishing companies. Several of his publications appear in journals and books that are available only on the Internet, including *LIBRES: Library and Information Science Research Electronic Journal, Excellence in Teaching*, and teach-psych.org.

1 Catching the Writing Bug and Doing Something With It

Festus E. Obiakor, Bob Algozzine,
and Jeffrey P. Bakken

Revelation

We make ourselves a place apart
Behind light words that tease and flout,
But oh, the agitated heart
Till someone really finds us out.
'Tis pity if the case require
(Or so we say) that in the end
We speak the literal to inspire
The understanding of a friend.
But so with all, from babes that play
At hide-and-seek to God afar,
So all who hide too well away
Must speak and tell us where they are.

~ Robert Frost

Robert Frost's poem, "Revelation" (Lathem, 1969, p. 19), challenges our agitated hearts to reveal themselves. We all have had the urge to show our intentions on various issues in some form or fashion. Scholars, educators, and students always have had good ideas, but the worry is often why, how, or where they should share them. In respective communities, great orators and storytellers are consistently misrepresented as their stories pass from person to person. In other words, our stories are told one dimensionally when we only use speech to reveal our hearts' agitations. Spooner, Algozzine, Thurlow, Obiakor, and Heller (1997) noted that "no amount of discourse or rhetoric can remediate the inconsistencies in our history, values, and stories unless we write them down" (p. 19).

The urge to tell stories through writing is an intriguing phenomenon. Busy schedules with frequent daily demands weaken the urge and the action.

We acknowledge that producing a written product for dissemination can be a very difficult task, but we also know that this is a very important endeavor that is essential to the advancement of knowledge. Because it is sometimes so difficult, many make excuses even when they have wonderful ideas to share. Henson (1995) wrote:

> Whether or not you are aware of your strengths, all workers perform some parts of their jobs exceptionally well. This means that you have information that is valuable to others who hold similar positions. But, month after month and year after year, aspiring writers attend writing workshops and openly acknowledge that they do not believe they have anything worthy of publication. This conclusion is unwise and it is wrong. You do have knowledge that is worth sharing, and until you acknowledge this truth you will remain unduly handicapped. (p. 29)

It is common knowledge that some issues and/or topics are closer to people's hearts than others. Because their likes and dislikes as human beings motivate them to attach different values to things, they can contribute to debates on those issues through writing. If people step outside their comfort zone and try writing about new topics less familiar to them, this can be an exciting new way to learn about areas that are less familiar to them. We are convinced that people can catch the writing bug; however, the critical issue continues to be why or how they spend their writing time. Our reactions to the possibilities are the major thrusts of this chapter.

WHY CATCH THE WRITING BUG?

Professionals who spend their time teaching and learning with others constantly have the urge to tell stories and share experiences. They also understand that these experiences will be inconsistently interpreted unless they share them in writing. To better understand these behaviors, consider some reasons for catching the writing bug.

Write to Be Empowered

Writing is empowering. Self-knowledge and self-esteem are important variables; however, self-ideal is built through self-empowerment (Obiakor, Stile, & Muller, 1994). To be self-empowered, people must be cognizant of current issues confronting them. Many professionals try to share ideas at professional conferences, often discovering great networking milieus that assist in disseminating ideas. Unfortunately, these same people sometimes become "gun-shy" when it comes to writing. People need to take advantage of networking and capitalize on these meetings. One way to do this is to collaborate on a topic of mutual interest. Thanks to technology, this has become an easy and acceptable practice. Writing alone can be difficult and sometimes getting started is the hardest part of all. Henson (2005b) identified six personal myths that haunt potential writers:

- I'm not sure I have what it takes.
- I don't have time to write.
- I don't have anything worth writing about.
- The editors will reject my manuscript because my name is not familiar to them.
- My vocabulary and writing skills are too limited.
- In my field there are few opportunities to publish. (pp.17–19)

The previous myths are very dangerous because of their ramifications on personal self-worth. It does not take much to have an idea to share with colleagues—the only difference this time is that these ideas are to be shared in writing. For instance, we had ideas for a book of this nature; we decided to share them in writing, and we involved colleagues who were also willing to share their ideas in writing. Often myths are nonproductive alibis. The truth is that all of us make time for whatever we like to do. In addition, we all try our best in whatever we feel motivated to do. Writing is no different. If you like writing and need to do it for your career, you must allocate time to writing.

Although some colleagues have had the urge to tell their stories, some have told us that they do not write because there is nothing new to write about. For some it is the fear of rejection, but we learn from that as well. Feedback from others is just one way to become a better writer. Some even challenge the quality of books and articles published by others. But, as the adage goes, "one person's junk is another person's treasure." Our experiences and ideas in this chapter might not make sense to one reader but they might be very valuable to others. Henson (1995) indicated that "some people enjoy just sitting around talking about writing, telling why they don't write for publication. . . . Others talk a lot about writing they plan to do, but they never get around to it" (p. 2). He added that "the world is full of people who dream about becoming something they aren't but who haven't the initiative to become whatever they wish to become" (p. 3). To become a writer you must write (Henson, 1993, 1995, 1999, 2001, 2003, 2005a, 2005b). Everyone has something to share and should do so through writing.

Write to Manifest Energies of Freedom

To manifest our energies of freedom through writing, most people must go beyond the usual talk to action. Some years ago, Lorch (1981) explained that "the process of writing involves bringing together three separate and distinct elements and establishing relationships between and among them" (p. 32). These triangular elements are (a) the writer, (b) the reader, and (c) the subject matter. Bridges and Lunsford (1984) confirmed

- That writing is a powerful means of learning. Through writing, the writer refines his/her thinking. He/she toys with ideas; ideas toy with him/her.
- That writing is a recursive act that most often proceeds not smoothly but it fits and starts as the writer struggles to find meaning.
- That writing must be marked by significance. Thus, the writer's task is to reveal his/her insight into a particular topic to the reader.
- That form is a function of meaning. (p. v)

The positive energies all of us manifest as human beings are based on how we unmask ourselves. Many of us unmask ourselves through writing and in the process derive freedom. According to Henson (1999)

> You can decide *what* you want to write, *when* you want to write it, and even *where* you want to write. Authors can even choose their audiences. Writing offers opportunity to earn recognition. Few professionals enjoy more admiration than successful writers. Most people also know that writing *offers authors an opportunity to apply their creative talents*. When you write, you invent; and then you share your creation with as many others as possible. *Our society places much value on creativity.* (p. 3)

Write to Be on the Cutting Edge of Issues

Writing helps many to be on the cutting edge of issues. Others bridge the gap between researchers and practitioners through writing. Additionally, in any field, practitioners have a lot to say and write about. Spooner and Heller (1993) remarked that "the lingering problem is the translation gap between the usual author (teacher educator) and the relevant audience (teacher), a gap between research and practice" (p. 47). The irony is that teachers are knowledgeable about what works in the classroom even though they are the target audience of most educational publications. Spooner and Heller emphasized that teachers "should publish because they have much to gain as both author and audience" (pp. 47-48). Teachers often don't realize that writing about what they do and how they do it could benefit others around the world. Practice publications are as beneficial as research-based publications and all types of authors should be accepted and acknowledged. Written documents help to bridge historical gaps; "writing is the full manifestation of discourse" (Ricoeur, 1976, pp. 25-26). In addition, "when stories are passed orally from person to person their accuracy begins to dwindle, but when they are written, they endure the test of time" (Spooner et al., 1997, p. 18). Past, present, and future practices are connected through written documents. Simply put, writing advances history, and history advances writing; in this context, writing is a continuous, ever-renewing effort to push back the frontiers of ignorance. It is both art and science and all aspects of it are equally rewarding.

Write for Intrinsic and Extrinsic Rewards

In colleges and universities, the predominant debate is whether teaching, scholarship, or service should be given top priority in continuing, tenuring, promoting, and rewarding faculty. The debate usually focuses on what the mission of a college/university is or ought to be. The person most referenced in these campus debates is Ernest Boyer (the late President of the Carnegie Foundation for the Advancement of Teaching), who consistently challenged higher education to reconceptualize its definition of scholarship. Boyer (1994) wrote

> I'm concerned that in recent years, higher education's historic commitment to service seems to have diminished. I'm troubled that many now view the campus as a place where professors get tenured and students get credentialed; the overall efforts of the academy are not considered to be at the vital center of the nation's work. And what I find disturbing is the growing feeling in this country that higher education is a private benefit, not a public good. (p. A48)

We have great respect for Dr. Boyer's work and comments. We, too, have great concern about the direction of America's higher education. People need less confusion and more consistency. Boyer shared his ideas not only orally, but also in writing. He published many books, monographs, journal articles, and newsletter materials. In fact, in some quarters, he has been viewed as one of the renowned scholars of the 20th century. We suggest that people do what Boyer did. For example, if your creativity lies in teaching, share your creative ideas about teaching with colleagues in writing—people are always searching for innovative teaching strategies. We believe teaching, scholarly, and service activities go (and should go) hand in hand. They are not mutually exclusive, they are mutually inclusive. How can teachers be "great" teachers if they are not current in their field? Also, how can teachers be "great" teachers if their teachings are incorrect and archaic? The legitimacy of what is being taught is derived from current scholarship evaluated and authenticated by peers. Action, accountability, and achievement keep us current.

Writing has both intrinsic and extrinsic rewards. Personally, we are excited when we see our names in print and when our works are acknowledged or used by others. There is usually no end to this excitement, whether it is the first publication or not. That excitement, on its own merit, can be motivating and empowering. Through writing, we earn the respect of colleagues, students, and the professionals who interact with us. For example, our experiences have shown that students respect professors who use their published works as handouts for instruction. Additionally, professors earn tenure and promotion because of their scholarly contributions to the field. Spooner et al. (1997) reiterated

> Many university programs survive because of the writing efforts of their faculties. Funded grant proposals and manuscripts published in professional journals provide evidence of successful writing efforts. Most proposals will not be funded unless they are well written and well targeted to address current problems. Some knowledge base and technical skills are required to produce a good grant proposal. Results of these grants are in turn published as books, book chapters, and research articles to increase visibility. (p. 19)

HOW TO CATCH THE WRITING BUG

All of us have something important to say; and because of it, we also have something important to write about. The critical question is, how do we go about writing? Although there is no one model to follow, there are specific styles (e.g., American Psychological Association) to which writers must adhere. The act and process of writing must be known and put into practice (see Tip 1.1). Lorch (1981) explained that

> the act of writing is a process made up of understandable parts. It is not a mysterious flow of words from pens. An understandable process can be taught and learned. Everyone who writes effectively learned at one time how to do it. (p. 6)

The process of professional sharing involves (a) picking a topic that you think has potential and asking questions to generate information you may use in your writing, (b) sketching a tentative purpose and structure for your writing, (c) selecting and analyzing your audience, and (d) writing your draft in light of your purpose and choice of audience (Becker & Richards, 2007; Bridges & Lunsford, 1984; Heinrich, 2008; Henson, 1999; Obiakor, Lomotey, & Rueda, 1997).

Know your story with style.

TIP
1.1

You need to know your topic or theme of interest and pursue it in detail. Not only must you know your topic, you must also know the act and process of writing (e.g., know the style foundations expected for academic writing).

It is important to understand that you must pursue the writing bug in order to catch it. You must not be "gun-shy" about unmasking yourself through writing (see Tip 1.2). As Henson (1999) pointed out

- The competition among writers is keen. To succeed, writers must write excellently.
- Good writers are self-made, not born. By learning a few hard facts, you can master the skills needed to succeed in writing.
- Successful writing for nonfiction magazines, journals, and books requires—above everything else—the ability to write clearly.
- Plain, simple writing is preferred over sophisticated, esoteric, pompous writing.
- Successful writers are well organized. They have designated times and places for writing.
- In our busy society, nobody *makes* or *finds* the time to write. Successful writers assign a higher priority to writing than to other activities.
- Clear goals give writers direction and incentive.
- Self-discipline and self-motivation characterize successful writers. You are the only one who can give yourself the kick in the pants that is needed to get started. (pp. 21-22)

Unmask yourself through writing.

TIP
1.2

Enjoy your freedom and use your creative talents to create ideas. Do not be "gun-shy." You maximize your potential when you understand the connection between writing and freedom.

Writing involves hard work and dedication. No writer writes perfectly the first time; it helps to view writing as an attitude, not as a job. It becomes a stressor when we view it as a compulsory job—it loses its fun. Spooner and Heller (1993) stated that "a 25-page paper of publishable quality does not automatically or easily appear on the page because one wishes it to be there" (p. 48). In writing, you can be your own worst enemy. Many people talk about publishing in what they call the "top journal," and we all have friends like them (see Tip 1.3). In reality, procrastination and ego are counterproductive to writing. As Spooner and Heller contended, to write productively, we must (a) be at our physical best, (b) manage our writing environment, (c) keep track of our ideas, (d) let our ideas flow, (e) use an outline, and (f) write the first draft.

TIP
1.3

Talk less and write more.

Let your writing do the talking. Avoid the "victim" mentality and empower yourself through writing. Set your priorities straight. Do not make writing your stressor. Have fun!

Through the years, we all have mentored many people in writing. We have discovered that many professionals put off writing until they want to get either tenure or promotion. The fact remains that people grow in writing by writing—there is no magic formula that will solve all writing problems. Writers just need to write, sometimes with others as we have done in this chapter (see Tip 1.4). To become a better writer, (a) study a topic intensively, (b) confront challenging and important issues, (c) conduct systematic work with colleagues, (d) write clearly and with style, (e) embrace feedback, and (f) do not lose your perspective (Algozzine, Obiakor, & Spooner, 1997; Becker & Richards, 2007; Henson, 1993, 1995, 1999, 2001, 2003, 2005a, 2005b; Kiewra, 1994; Obiakor et al., 1997).

TIP
1.4

Collaborate with colleagues in your writing.

Involve people in your writing projects because "two heads are better than one." Colleagues might add new perspectives to your thinking. By writing with other people, you advance the context of history, and the context of history advances you.

PERSPECTIVE

We are all agitated hearts with something to say or share. Why and how we should share our ideas continues to interest and intrigue us. We argue in this chapter that if people respond to agitations through speech alone, their stories will be told unidimensionally. We also suggest that no amount of rhetoric can remediate the inconsistencies in our stories unless we write them down. We are not born writers—we learn to write by writing.

Our experiences tell us that anybody can catch the writing bug. Positive thinking is an important key. The time spent "talking big" or "knocking down" other people's works could be spent on productive writing activities. Planning is also important. Writing is a skill that requires hard work, dedication, and the "write" attitude. Check your own attitude and skills about writing (cf. Algozzine, Spooner, & Karvonen, 2002; Henson, 2005b; Podsen, 1997; Rafanello, 2008):

- Is fear of writing interfering with your perceptions (and those of others) of your professional progress, effectiveness, and success?
- Is reluctance to write based on self-perception of skills or other beliefs?
- What would make writing easier for you?
- What would change your perceptions in the direction of more productive writing?

Writing should not be viewed as a stressful job. Most of us cannot afford to put off writing until it is time for tenure or promotion. When we do this, we become our own worst enemies. Writing needs to be a part of a person's culture and projects should always be ongoing to keep motivated, fresh, and ready for the promotion/tenure cycle. Although there is no one formula for writing, you can do some things to make your writing better. Henson (1993) suggested that we (a) write captivating titles, (b) use subheadings to capture attention, (c) write fluidly, (d) write simply, (e) write assertively, and (f) show application. We must try to know our audience, the readers. In addition, it pays to write with others—they add multiple voices. We conclude with the words of Lewis and Sugai (1996), "before you sit down to write, identify one or two important points you would like to make, who your audience will be, and what information the reader will need to replicate your idea or critically analyze your point" (p. 16). The points we tried to make here are (a) There are many reasons to catch the writing bug and all of them are important to professional educators, and (b) there are many ways to catch the writing bug and all of them are within the reach of all professional educators.

REFERENCES

Algozzine, B., Obiakor, F. E., & Spooner, F. (1997, April). *Writing for publication.* Paper presented at the Council for Exceptional Children Annual International Convention, Salt Lake City, UT.

Algozzine, B., Spooner, F., & Karvonen, M. (2002). *How to prepare a research article in APA style.* Arlington, VA: Council for Exceptional Children.

Becker, H. S., & Richards, P. (2007). *Writing for social scientists: How to start and finish your thesis, book, or article* (2nd ed.). Chicago: University of Chicago Press.

Boyer, E. L. (1994, March 9). Creating the new American college. *The Chronicle of Higher Education,* p. A48.

Bridges, C. W., & Lunsford, R. F. (1984). *Writing: Discovering form and meaning.* Belmont, CA: Wadsworth.

Heinrich, K. T. (2008). *A nurse's guide to presenting and publishing: Dare to share.* Sudbury, MA: Jones and Bartlett.

Henson, K. T. (1993). Six ways to capture and hold the attention of nonfiction readers. *Writers' Journal, 14,* 19-20.

Henson, K. T. (1995). *The art of writing for publication.* Needham Heights, MA: Allyn & Bacon.

Henson, K. T. (1999). Writing for professional publication. Needham Heights, MA: Allyn & Bacon.

Henson, K. T. (2001). Writing for professional journals: Paradoxes and promises. *Phi Delta Kappan, 82,* 765-768.

Henson, K. T. (2003). Writing for professional publication: Some myths and some truths. *Phi Delta Kappan, 84,* 788-791.

Henson, K. T. (2005a). Writing for publication: A controlled art. *Phi Delta Kappan, 86,* 777-781.

Henson, K. T. (2005b). *Writing for publication: Steps to academic success.* Boston: Allyn & Bacon.

Kiewra, K. A. (1994). A slice of advice. *Educational Researcher, 23,* 31-33.

Lathem, E. C. (Ed. 1969). *The poetry of Robert Frost.* New York: Holt, Rinehart and Winston.

Lewis, T. J., & Sugai, C. M. (1996). A guide to preparing manuscripts for publication. *Beyond Behavior, 7,* 16-17.

Lorch, S. (1981). *Basic writing: A practical approach.* Cambridge, MA: Winthrop.

Obiakor, F. E., Lomotey, K., & Rueda, R. (1997, January). *Writing for publication.* Paper presented at the Multicultural Symposium of the Division for Culturally and Linguistically Diverse Exceptional Learners, the Council for Exceptional Children, New Orleans, LA.

Obiakor, F. E., Stile, S. W, & Muller, D. (1994). Self-concept in school programs: Conceptual and research foundations. In F. E. Obiakor & S. W. Stile (Eds.), *Self-concepts of exceptional learners: Current perspectives for educators* (pp. 1-18). Dubuque, IA: Kendall/Hunt.

Podsen, I. J. (1997). *Written expression: The principal's survival guide.* Larchmont, NY: Eye on Education.

Rafanello, D. (2008). Writing well: It's all about attitude. *Exchange, 181,* 58-59.

Ricoeur, P. (1976). *Interpretation theory: Discourse and the surplus of meaning.* Fort Worth: The Texas Christian University Press.

Spooner, F., Algozzine, B., Thurlow, M. L., Obiakor, F. E., & Heller, H. W. (1997). Ethnic minority scholars writing for professional publication: From myth to reality. *Multiple Voices, 2,* 12-20.

Spooner, F., & Heller, H. W. (1993). Writing for publication in journals for practitioners: Suggestions for teachers and early career researchers. *Remedial and Special Education, 14,* 47-52.

2 WRITING, PROFESSIONAL DEVELOPMENT, AND BEING KNOWN FOR WHAT YOU DO

Bob Algozzine, Fred Spooner, and
Anne Bauer

I was brought up to believe
that the only thing worth doing
was to add to the sum
of accurate information
in the work!

~ Margaret Mead

In practically every institution of higher education, there are explicit or implied policies and procedures that assist and, perhaps, even direct the process of professional development of individual faculty. So that a coherent message is broadcast to faculty about expected and accepted professional behavior and what related contingencies of promotion and tenure entail, department and college policies are usually in line with visions, missions, and ambitions at the university level. In some of these documents, there may be general statements of broad expectations such as supporting the efforts and programs of the college appropriate to one's role; demonstrating integrity and high standards of ethical and professional behavior; and being collegial, collaborative, human, and respectful of diversity. At a more precise level, there are likely to be statements which facilitate the definition of teaching, service, and research activities that help shape and direct all professional development activities.

For most professors in higher education, teaching is the basis for employment. It typically involves such activities as providing content area instruction, advising students, and supervising practical classroom experiences as well as student-directed scholarship. Professional development in teaching is usually supported by supplying a statement about one's teaching philosophy, demonstrating expertise and currency in the content area of one's assigned courses, incorporating instructional technology into teaching, and assessing instruction via peer and student evaluation.

Applying knowledge in one's field beyond the university classroom provides opportunities for professional development. Generally, these service activities occur in three areas:

- Service to the profession (e.g., roles in governance of professional state and national association such as the Council for Exceptional Children, CEC, or one of its divisions; serving on the editorial board of a professional journal such as *Teacher Education and Special Education,* the journal of the Teacher Education Division, TED, of CEC);
- Service to practitioners and community (e.g., local CEC chapters and local schools);
- Service to the institution such as serving on departmental committees (e.g., search committees for new positions), college committees (e.g., tenure and promotion committees), universitywide committees (e.g., committee on distance learning).

Evidence to evaluate service is typically represented by some of the following activities: sustained involvement in professional organizations and associations in one's field at state, regional, national, and international levels; contributions to professional organizations or associations that are focused and that draw upon one's professional expertise; and leadership in addressing important issues relevant to one's profession.

Research usually means expanding the knowledge base in one's field (e.g., severe disabilities, behavior disorders, and mild mental retardation) with scholarship and professional writing that synthesizes and integrates extant information or disseminates the results of experimental or quasi-experimental studies. Evidence to support research activity is usually provided by a clearly articulated research agenda and focus; a documentation of collaboration with colleagues, including junior faculty, in efforts to expand the knowledge in their respective fields; and a sustained record of scholarship and professional writing reflecting systematic efforts to conduct, report, and disseminate empirical research.

Most new and experienced professors have little trouble compiling teaching and service records that are valued by their university peers. Typically, teaching assignments are distributed systematically to faculty with expertise in program areas. Similarly, service opportunities are everywhere. The area that presents more concern and less certainty is research. Too often, young and experienced faculty members are provided little guidance in designing and sustaining a research agenda, developing collaborative relations, and meeting reasonable publication standards. On the other hand, research is often the most potent variable in the professional development equation, and levels of anxiety rise disproportionately with levels of uncertainty associated with scholarship, professional writing, and research.

In this chapter, we focus on two areas that we believe support professional development productivity: the importance of integrating teaching, service, and research activities and some guidelines that maximize efforts in scholarship and professional writing.

INTEGRATION IS KEY TO SUCCESS

Many who have been successful in higher education are those who have found a way to integrate their teaching, research, and service, so that these activities are not discrete and unrelated experiences. Those individuals who excel have been able to find and establish an integrated focus for their professional careers. The people who are successful are those who usually have a relatively clear idea about how to make their research, teaching, and service support one another. At a basic level, an individual with doctoral level training—let's say in the area of severe disabilities—would more than likely teach courses in the area of severe disabilities and would not teach courses in the area of the gifted. A person with expertise in the area of severe disabilities would likely belong to professional organizations such as CEC's division on Developmental Disabilities and TASH (formerly, The Association for Persons with Severe Handicaps). From a teacher education perspective, that same individual might also belong to CEC's TED. This professional would likely try to carve out his or her specialty niche in professional associations, seek to participate not only in their annual meetings as a way to present research findings, but likely also serve on various committees within these organizations as a way to engage in relevant service as part of career development activities. The research agenda for this individual could proceed in one of a number of different directions which relate to persons with severe disabilities.

The research paradigm (e.g., qualitative or quantitative) that one adopts is to some significant degree, based on what one studies and the research tools that were likely used to complete one's dissertation (e.g., single subject design vs. a group design). Although most researchers typically know one of the research paradigms very well, they should not rule out the possibility of expanding their ability to approach a research question. Let the question at hand, in part, dictate which type of research method best addresses the question under investigation. In many cases, working with other colleagues—those who are like-minded, and perhaps, some who pursue research from different perspectives—will help to expand one's knowledge about research designs. Often, if a research question is carefully phrased and the study precisely articulated, the experimental outcomes under analysis will yield insight for the next experimental investigation (Johnston & Pennypacker, 1980, 1993). Maybe there is not an individual who is interested in your research question, per se; someone may be interested in assisting with designing the next study, with a particular set of analyses in mind. In most instances, working with a team maximizes the effort. Members of the team can decide their respective roles in the current investigation or multiple investigations, including who will do what and when (e.g., who will take the lead on which manuscripts, who will write conference proposals to be submitted for potential presentations, and which organizations the research group will target for the next academic year). Perhaps there are individuals with whom you went to school who are now employed at different spots around the country who have similar programmatic and research interests as you. Just because you are no longer at the same physical location does not preclude the opportunity to collaborate. It may make it somewhat more difficult, but with e-mail and the ability to share working documents online, collaborating with a colleague from another university (even if it is three time zones away, or halfway around the world), is possible. As your professional career develops, you may even cultivate collegial relationships with individuals you meet at association meetings. You attended their presentation at a conference, and made a judgment that they do good work—not only that they do good work, but are interested in the same topic. You make arrangements to speak with them, a research agenda is crafted, roles and responsibilities are delineated, and a partnership is forged.

Being able to conduct, report, and disseminate research is an important component of a productive professional development portfolio. A good rule of thumb to follow in academia is: Think twice about the activity that is pursued, and if you can't write about it, present it, or make it fit into the rest of your professional expectations, think twice about whether it is really worth doing. Each component of a professional development portfolio of research, teaching, and service should complement each other. Decisions about how you spend your time as a professor need to be carefully crafted, so that each piece fits together as part of the whole. You must always consider how these parts fit together. How can service complement research? How can research enhance teaching? Always take into account how the activities in which you engage can be documented, how each integrates with the larger picture, and above all, how, if you do it, you can write about it: Does what you are doing have the potential to become a manuscript or product that can be used as evidence of professional productivity?

Scholarship and professional writing are, in many cases, the most important part of a faculty member's tenure and promotion dossier because publications are widely respected as evidence of advancement of knowledge. Members of the respective departmental review committees are usually knowledgeable of the important journals in one's discipline, and such contributions can be evaluated (quantitatively and qualitatively). A quick review of publications and articles in press can readily reveal gaps in a candidate's writing record, or trends that expose periods of relative inactivity, followed by bursts of attempts at writing as a mandated review approaches, or balance in published material over the long haul. Although teaching and service are complementary components to one's professional career, this is academia, not a position in public service nor is it a teaching role at a local community college; scholarship, professional writing, and the generation of new knowledge are highly valued.

For many underrepresented faculty groups (i.e., women and minorities) who lack strong support bases, the pragmatic response to the question, "Why publish?" could simply be to remain employed. Besides this practical response, Hardin (1991) and Hartman (1991) concurred that women need to research and publish to generate new ways of knowing and thinking. For instance, women faculty may not be taken seriously nor respected for their contributions to the field without publication. As Obiakor, Ford, and Mutua ask in Chapter 3 of this book, "Who will tell your stories correctly in writing if you do not?" Women need, and have, justifiable grounds for claims to tell fewer false stories about gender, social relations, nature, and reality. For these related reasons, women and other underrepresented faculty groups should view scholarship as a gender and cultural imperative.

MAKING THE MOST OF SCHOLARSHIP AND PROFESSIONAL WRITING

If a report is to be submitted or a manuscript is to be published, it must first be written. Words, phrases, sentences, paragraphs, and sections of a written product just do not magically appear on the page. Usually trying to find the time to write does not produce manuscripts either. Writing takes discipline.

For most professors in higher education there are many competing priorities in one's professional life—let alone those things in one's personal life that also compete for time in one's daily schedule. From a professional perspective, there are lectures to prepare, classes to teach, students to advise, papers to grade, an e-mail and phone messages to answer. With all of these activities, and perhaps even others, how does one find the time to write? We could say that it is really quite straight-forward: *one simply must make the time*. Writing requires disciplined time management.

Those in higher education who have not only survived but actually flourished under the publishing contingencies of the academy have somehow found a way. Although there are probably some similarities to many of the success stories that you are likely to hear from your colleagues, the formula is based on individual need. Consider a few examples. Everybody has a colleague (Dr. X) who thrives on 11th-hour "crash and burn" activities. Dr. X always manages to "get the job done," but there is always plenty of doubt in the minds of those with whom Dr. X works. Dr. X's opposite-end-of-the-continuum colleague (Dr. C) systematically steps from the beginning to the end of a project with the precision and timing of a well-executed symphony. Dr. C has a place for everything and the only problem is deciding what project to do first. Similarly, some folks are morning people, and others tend to do their best work at the opposite end of the clock; some find that their office at the university, after the bulk of the regular workday is completed, meetings are finished, and most of their colleagues have gone home, is the place where they write. Others work at home where they have a professional space, perhaps even an office with all the comforts of a well-designed work area, better than the one provided by the university.

There is no magic in successful writing. The key is maximizing effort, which is not a new idea (cf. Henson, 1993, 1995, 1997, 1999, 2001, 2003, 2005a, 2005b; Skinner, 1981; Spooner, Algozzine, Thurlow, Obiakor, & Heller, 1997; Spooner & Heller, 1993). This chapter is grounded in the work of Skinner and supports five maxims: (a) Put yourself in the best place for writing; (b) Stay away from connected prose as long as possible; (c) Take advantage of technology, but do not be controlled by it; (d) Model the successful behavior of others; and (e) Do not give up because of failure or rest on success.

Put Yourself in the Best Place for Writing

First, a little exercise, adequate rest, and an appropriate diet can't hurt. We usually do not do our best work when we are tired, either mentally, physically, or both. A daily schedule that includes some time away from writing, the amount of sleep that is appropriate for you, a little nourishment to refuel the system, and some type of exercise can go a long way to freshen your perspective on professional tasks. Next in that daily schedule, you must make some time for writing. As discussed earlier, morning, afternoon, evening, or after midnight, it doesn't matter, as long as it works for you. It is a good idea to let your output help you evaluate what times work best (see Tip 2.1).

Once you have established a place and a time to write, practice in the location. Take time to arrange your books and your professional journals, get the appropriate files on the hard drive of your computer, and make sure to backup your information daily. There will be occasions when you are away from your desk and you get an idea about the piece that you are currently developing. Ideas need time to percolate.

TIP
2.1

Identify a writing lifestyle that works for you.
Much like you might develop a budget when thinking about what to do with your money, make some systematic decisions about what to do with your time. This means making decisions about personal as well as professional time. A familiar adage begins "all work and no play"—and it should ring true in planning your writing lifestyle.

Stay Out of Prose as Long as Possible

Writing is thinking written down. The essence of writing is rewriting. The essence of rewriting is thinking about writing. Writing is a continuous process. All writing begins with a "blank slate." For many, the most difficult stage of writing is producing the first complete, cogent sentence. Fear of failure, perils of perfectionism, and paralysis by analysis make many reluctant to put those first words on paper. Remember, writing is thinking written down. To facilitate the transition from thoughts to written products, it helps to keep track of ideas that come to you when you are not at your desk but still thinking about writing. Your "brainstorms" may come when you are driving in the car, as you are walking to class, and even as you are setting the table for dinner—or at some other, seemingly odd time. You must create a mechanism to capture those ideas, jot them down on a scrap of paper, or have an official "list of notes." The notes do not have to be the beginning of a formal document. They are just notes, written in some hieroglyphic that perhaps only you understand. The important thing is that you have written enough, and made it legible enough, that when you look at what you have written, at some later point in time, you can capture or recapture the essence of your idea.

At this point, the ideas should trigger phrases, the phrases sentences, the sentences paragraphs, and the paragraphs products. The form and shape may follow a typical research article with the standard sections of abstract, introduction, method, results, and discussion as its components or become the filler for an outline (Algozzine, Spooner, & Karvonen, 2002; Fuchs & Fuchs, 1993). It is a good idea to take the writing task one component at a time. Assuming that the data are already analyzed and you are well aware of the outcomes, begin to jot down information for the introductory section, taking into account the three or four major studies that have laid the groundwork for the current piece of research. It is now a matter of highlighting the salient pieces of those studies and delineating how your work stems from them. Get the points down first, go back later and build in the transitions, from one paragraph to the next, from one study to the next. There may be additional ideas that come to you that could potentially fit in the discussion section; keep track of those on your note pad.

As the points appear, you should begin to see how one point relates to the next, and how the points relate to the whole. At this stage a final product begins to develop. As with the notes, nothing formal is in order. You must check to see if what you have written relates one point to the next, and then see if all of the necessary points are included. After you have written a chapter or manuscript, list the title, headings, and subheadings on a separate sheet of paper exactly as they appear in the body of the text. You can use this "reverse outline" to check to be sure that similar level headings reflect similar levels of content importance. Writing is thinking written down, putting thoughts on paper, rewriting, and thinking about what you have written (see Tip 2.2). Avoid fears of failure, perils of perfectionism, and paralysis by analysis: Just write and rewrite until you get it right!

TIP
2.2

Think of all your writing as a work in progress.
Don't spend too much time writing the perfect title, sentence, paragraph, page, or document. Work from ideas that you accumulate on paper. Take those ideas that are accruing and begin to develop them into a product. When the product is done, review it to be sure it presents the message you wanted.

Take Advantage of Technology, But Don't Be Controlled by It

Technology is changing our lives. Routine writing tasks like outlining, editing, and revising take less time today, and they are simply easier than ever before in history. Paradigm shifts occur in the field of technology every 18 months; important changes occur more frequently. To keep up, you must go with the flow. Do not use an out-of-date application if a greatly improved, more powerful one comes along. You must be prepared to upgrade to improve your writing lifestyle, and an overall productivity shift will happen.

Many faculty members at any college or university were "paper trained"; that is, they were taught to write using a pencil and paper, and then expected to give their work to someone else to type. Or they prepared a handwritten draft of a document or portions of a document and then typed it themselves. Think of all the extra effort expended! For all practical purposes, they were doing the work twice (i.e., writing it down and then typing it). In the age of information technology and personal computers, this would appear to be a sound and prudent decision. If you do not have a computer, get one. If you do not already know how to type and compose at the keyboard, learn or develop another strategy for editing and revising your work. If you still need the paper to be more productive, do your editing and rewriting on printed copies of manuscripts.

Of course, writing involves more than putting the fingers to the keyboard and sending some form of coherent visual output to a screen. It also means reviewing what has been written, reading material that relates to what you are writing, and maybe even locating additional resources. On any writing project, it makes sense to include time away from the machine. Remember, it is a machine and you control what it does (see Tip 2.3).

TIP
2.3

Tip 2.3: Use technologies to improve your writing.
The Internet is a powerful writing resource. In addition to searching for information on specific topics and educational journals, there are dozens of Web sites where you can find self-help information on writing. Here are just a few: On-line Resources for Writers: http://webster.comment.edu/writing/writing.htm, Writer's Workshop: http://www.cws.illinois.edu/workshop/writers/, and Elements of Style: http://www.bartleby.com/141/.

Model Others' Successful Behavior

If you are writing a manuscript for publication in a professional journal, check recent issues for author guidelines or obtain a copy from the editor or publisher. This information is readily available on Web pages of professional associations and publishers (e.g., http://www.heldref.org/jermanu.php). Although they may not be very specific about what will be published, they typically offer broad advice regarding content and style that can be very helpful in preparing your work. They also provide guidelines for completing the submission process. It is a good idea to find two or three written products that you like and use them as models for your own work. What you write should be your own words, but reviewing recent issues of the journal you are considering as a publication source for something you have written can be very helpful in putting it all together.

Although it is generally considered more acceptable in the tenure and promotion stream to have published in notable refereed journals in your field, you should not avoid other sources. The more you write, the better you will be at writing, and a written product is better than no product at all. Small subscription journals that are highly focused in content coverage can be excellent sources for something you have written. Similarly, the reviews you receive from such a submission can go a long way in helping you improve your work for another journal. If you are just beginning a writing career, it is usually a good idea to begin with "less powerful" journals; it might be frustrating to begin with a tough journal like *Exceptional Children* or a similar journal focused heavily on research and characterized by a high rejection rate (see Tip 2.4). It is a good idea to contact editors for information about acceptance rates, special issues, or turnaround time if you cannot find it in the journal. The more information you have about what has been published (i.e., successful models), the better prepared you will be to write a successful publication (Henson, 1993, 1995, 1999, 2001, 2003, 2005a, 2005b).

TIP
2.4

Set goals you can easily achieve.
Nothing breeds failure like failure and nothing breeds success like success. Holding yourself to standards that are too high is a sure way to become an unsuccessful writer. Productive faculty engaged in teaching, service, and research typically publish three to five articles a year (some years more and some years less). Be reasonable, do not plan more than you can accomplish, but be sure you accomplish something and be proud of what you have done.

Do Not Give Up Because of Failure and Do Not Rest on Success

Writing is hard work and nothing makes hard work harder than failure. If something you write fails to be accepted, you must not give up on it. Successful writers respond favorably to rejection. They view it as an opportunity to improve what they have written. The essence of writing is rewriting. You must not get trapped by failures or successes in writing (see Tip 2.5). For women and other underrepresented faculty groups in higher education, their foci could be participatory and dialogic forms of writing if those are where their strengths lie. Do not give up! Use your intuition, collaborate, find a mentor, form or join a writing group—find out "what counts" and do it. For instance, if chapters do not support your attainment of tenure or promotion, explore other forms of publication. Find your voice, your style, and your genre.

TIP
2.5

Build on success; do not rest on it.
Even if something you have written is accepted without revisions, look for ways to extend, augment, and improve its message. Consider everything you have written a work in progress. Let your colleagues review your work and offer suggestions on how to improve it, even after it is published.

PERSPECTIVE

Sometimes you will write to give something back to your profession. Sometimes you will write to attempt to improve your profession. Sometimes you will write to improve your teaching. Sometimes you will write to advance your career. Whatever the reason, you can always improve your writing. Here are a few of life's little instructions to help along the way.

- Dream big dreams, but be known by what you write; written products are better than ideas regardless of why you produce them.
- Small works done are better than great works promised and undone; even the longest novel was written one word, sentence, paragraph, and page at a time.
- Spend time fixing problems rather than fixing blame; there are plenty of reasons for not writing. Avoid them like the plague.
- Do not separate who you are from what you write—by maintaining who you are, your contributions become unique.
- Unveil your hidden voice through writing.
- Avoid accepting assignments that won't be finished; nothing breeds accomplishment, confidence, and satisfaction like achievement and success.
- If you are not having fun writing, try writing something that is fun; commit yourself to quality, but remember there is a game to be played here.

As you live your professional development plan, build a portfolio (see Table 2.1 callout) of expected products and frequently monitor your progress. In addition to evidential documentation, include current indicators that support your work, including but not limited to:

- A clear narrative overview defining your professional goals and objectives in teaching, research, and service and summarizing in integrated statements evidence supporting your productivity, progress, and promise.

Table 2.1
Building a Professional Development Portfolio

Personal Information	Teaching	Research	Service

▪ Focus statement (terms, expectations, and conditions of employment)
 	
▪ Professional goals
 	
▪ Honors
  - Nominations
  - Awards
▪ Special opportunities
  - Reassignments
  - National recognition
	▪ Current teaching agenda
	
	▪ Past and present courses taught
	
	▪ Course evaluations
	  - Formal
	  - Informal
	  - Peer observations
	
	▪ Committees (related to teaching)
	  - University
	  - College
	  - Department
	  - Program
	  - External
	
	▪ Grant activity and Proposals (related to program development)
	
	▪ Advising
	
	▪ Scholarship
	
	▪ Supervision
	  - Independent studies
	  - Graduate student research/portfolios
	  - Co-publications
	  - Co-presentations
	
	▪ Special Opportunities
		▪ Current research agenda
		
		▪ Publications (books, chapters, articles, reports)
		  - In print
		  - In press
		▪ Work-in-progress
		
		▪ Grant activity and proposals (related to inquiry and research)
		
		▪ Conference presentations
		  - International
		  - National
		  - Regional
		  - State
		  - Local
		▪ Editorial services
		
		▪ Dissertation committees
		
		▪ Special Opportunities
			▪ Current service agenda
			
			▪ Institutional service
			  - University, college, and department committees
			  - Faculty
			  - governance
			  - Curriculum projects
			  - Accreditation support
			  - Group advising
			▪ Professional service
			  - Leadership
			  - Offices
			  - Committees
			  - Boards
			▪ Editorial reviews
			
			▪ Community service
			  - Federal projects
			  - SEA/LEA projects
			  - Task forces
			  - Workshops
			  - Professional development for practitioners
			▪ Special Opportunities

- A clear narrative overview defining your accomplishments in teaching and summarizing the collection of evidence available to support what you have done.
- A clear narrative overview defining your accomplishments in research and summarizing the collection of evidence available to support what you have done.
- A clear narrative overview defining your accomplishments in service and summarizing the collection of evidence available to support what you have done.

One thing we have learned after many years working and writing together is that the adage "different strokes for different folks" rings true when trying to pinpoint productive strategies of successful writers. To provide some indication of what works for at least one of us, we provide a brief case study illustration of a day in the life of a productive publishing professional.

Mornings at home surpass other times and locations as the best place for writing. Although travel (e.g., writing on airplanes en route to a conference presentation) can be somewhat conducive to writing (i.e., no phones to answer, no students to advise, and you really do not have to carry on much of a conversation with the person in the seat next to you), there is simply more room at home to create a lifestyle that works. Daily output can be printed to see how products composed at the keyboard look on paper. It is also easier to complete a daily writing session and then intersperse some time away from writing to take a break (e.g., go for a run) and think about what has been written (e.g., think about the big picture and how the most recent writing fits, develop new ideas that relate to the points being made in a paper, and prepare a mental outline). Typically, 2 or 3 hours a day are spent on writing projects before putting them away for the rest of the day. After going to the office, professional activities (e.g., committee meetings; responding to professional correspondence, voice mail, and e-mail; advising students; and preparing for class) other than writing take precedence, but there are plenty of opportunities to jot down thoughts and mental notes for the next day's writing. Classes scheduled in the late afternoon or evening make the morning writing lifestyle work well.

REFERENCES

Algozzine, B., Spooner, F., & Karvonen, M. (2002). *How to prepare a research article in APA style*. Arlington, VA: Council for Exceptional Children.

Fuchs, L., & Fuchs, D. (1993). Writing research reports for publication: Recommendations for new authors. *Remedial and Special Education, 14,* 39-46.

Hardin, S. (1991). Who knows? Identities and feminist epistemology. In J. E. Hartman & E. Messer-Davidow (Eds.), *(Engendering knowledge: Feminists in academe* (pp. 100–115). Knoxville, TN: University of Tennessee Press.

Hartman, J. E. (1991). Telling stories: The construction of women's agency. In J. E. Hartman & Messer-Davidow (Eds.), *(Engendering knowledge: Feminists in academe* (pp. 11-34). Knoxville, TN: University of Tennessee Press.

Henson, K. T. (1993). Six ways to capture and hold the attention of nonfiction readers. *Writers' Journal, 14,* 19-20.

Henson, K. T. (1995). *The art of writing for publication.* Needham Heights, MA: Allyn & Bacon.

Henson, K. T. (1997). Writing for publication: Some perennial mistakes. *Phi Delta Kappan, 78,* 781-784.

Henson, K. T. (1999). *Writing for professional publication.* Needham Heights, MA: Allyn & Bacon.

Henson, K. T. (2001). Writing for professional journals: Paradoxes and promises. *Phi Delta Kappan, 82,* 765-768.

Henson, K. T. (2003). Writing for professional publication: Some myths and some truths. *Phi Delta Kappan, 84,* 788-791.

Henson, K. T. (2005a). Writing for publication: A controlled art. *Phi Delta Kappan, 86,* 777-781.

Henson, K. T. (2005b). *Writing for publication: Road to academic achievement.* Boston: Allyn & Bacon.

Johnston, J. M., & Pennypacker, H. S. (1980). *Strategies and tactics of human behavior research.* Hillsdale, NJ: Erlbaum.

Johnston, J. M., & Pennypacker, H. S. (1993). *Strategies and tactics of behavioral research* (2nd ed.). Hillsdale, NJ: Erlbaum.

Skinner, B. F. (1981). How to discover what you have to say: A talk to students. *The Behavior Analyst, 4,* 1-8.

Spooner, F., Algozzine, B., Thurlow, M. L., Obiakor, F. E., & Heller, H. W. (1997). Ethnic minority scholars writing for professional publication: From myth to reality. *Multiple Voices, 2,* 12-20.

Spooner, F., & Heller, H. W. (1993). Writing for publication in journals for practitioners: Suggestions for teachers and early career researchers. *Remedial and Special Education, 14(3),* 47-52.

3
Expressing Culturally and Linguistically Diverse Scholar Voices

Festus E. Obiakor, Bridgie Alexis Ford, and Kagendo Mutua

Black at Last

Closely did I sit with my forefathers
Who patiently sacrificed for my freedom;
The coconut juice melted
like ice as it dripped slowly into my mouth;
The highway to the Egyptian Pyramid
seemed out of reach as I trekked
in the midst of the dreaded Crab-Bucket Syndrome;
Nearly did I hide my Blackness,
And, nearly did I hide my Brilliance;
My energy came back slowly and surely
as I continued my journey;
The distance got shorter and the sight of those
bamboo roofs reminded me of the Pyramid's creativity;
Black at last I was
as I touched the Egyptian Pyramid
built with Brilliance and Strength;
And I promised my forefathers,
Never again, and never again
will I hide my Blackness, Brilliance, and Beauty.

~ Festus E. Obiakor

In this poem, Obiakor (1998) highlighted the beauty and brilliance of his "Blackness," and acknowledged that perseverance, determination, and energy are needed to succeed in one's endeavors. In some fashion, he asked, "What would have happened had the creators of the Egyptian Pyramid discontinued their creative venture because of their predicaments (e.g., the hotness of the weather)?" "Where will our freedoms be today had our forebears given up due to hardships of slavery, colonization, and domination of the powers that be in the early years of the United States of America?" Throughout history, no freedom has ever been free; freedom results from commitment and sacrifice. In the same vein, writing involves personal commitment and sacrifice. In their classic book, *Current Issues and Enduring Questions*, Barnet and Bedau (1989) remarked that

> Despite what many people believe, writing is not only a method of putting one's ideas into words. Just as talking with others is a way of getting ideas, writing is a way of getting and developing ideas. Writing, in short, can be an important part of critical thinking. If fear of putting ourselves on record is the big reason we have trouble writing, another big reason is our fear that we have no ideas worth putting down But by jolting down notes- or even free associations- and by writing a draft, however weak, we can help ourselves to think our way toward good ideas. (p. 161)

Traditionally, books, monographs, journal and newspaper articles, and testing instruments are written to inform and to solve problems. However, they have failed to reflect cultural, linguistic, and historical values of ethnic minority members. Some culturally and linguistically diverse (CLD) group members have tried to set the record straight through writing. Sometimes, these efforts have not been respected or rewarded by colleagues, and to a large extent, many important historical facts continue to be missed in the literature. To this end, we ask one simple but critical question: Who will tell our stories correctly in writing if we do not? It is imperative that CLD scholars write not only for professional reasons but also for self-definition, self-identification, and self-pride. This is the major focus of this chapter. In addition, we share our experiences and provide tips for success in expressing diverse scholarly voices.

REASONS TO PUBLISH: CLD SCHOLAR PERSPECTIVES

There are many reasons to publish; however, for CLD scholars, there are three imperatives: (a) to create truths and respond to inaccuracies, (b) to advance career opportunities through self-determination, and (c) to exercise academic freedom. Responding to each enhances productivity for all.

Creating Truths and Responding to Inaccuracies

A scholar can be regarded as a seeker of truth. For those in general and special education, this process often entails redefining and creating paradigms to positively address multidimensional issues that confront children and youth from

CLD backgrounds and their families. The importance of researching and disseminating accurate information through publishing is clear (i.e., to address overall problems in education and recommend solutions). The historic and continued negative treatment given to CLD learners by general and special education systems makes the distribution of accurate information imperative (Ford, Obiakor, & Patton, 1995, Obiakor, 2007, 2008a; Obiakor & Beachum, 2005; Obiakor & Ford, 2002; Obiakor, Grant, & Dooley, 2002). The thorough examination of issues surrounding effective educational service delivery for CLD populations has been traditionally ignored, perceived as irrelevant, or addressed negatively by some non-CLD scholars (Littleton, 1995). It appears that biased and inaccurate research findings have dominated major journals in education. Unfortunately, these findings influence educational policies (e.g., federal-level decision making) and practices (see Littleton).

There has recently been increased focus on culturally and linguistically related issues in major educational journals and periodicals. Additionally, this era of great technological advances has ushered in online modalities for disseminating information, for instance through the creation of new important online journals, such as *Multicultural Learning and Teaching* (*MLT*). *MLT* is a highly regarded peer-reviewed journal that publishes scholarly articles on the multifaceted issues related to multicultural education. Through *MLT*, CLD scholars and "allied others" (Rogers & Swadener, 1999) have found an alternative outlet for the important work pertaining to multicultural issues in education. *MLT* and others like it are filling a niche in educational publishing by focusing exclusively on the issues that mainstream journals are apt to reject or marginalize. This, in turn, has increased the visibility of many CLD scholars who focus their works on alternative paradigms and practices for CLD children and youth with disabilities and/or gifts and talents. In spite of this visibility, systematic permeation has not occurred. We are strongly convinced that until CLD scholars deal with issues surrounding quality service delivery to CLD youth and their families, their perspectives will remain controllably invisible in significant journals. CLD scholars must take advantage of new outlets, challenge existing paradigms, and "debunk traditional perspectives through their work" (Obiakor & Algozzine, 2007, p. ii).

One of the tenets of critical race theory (CRT) addresses this very issue: that CLD scholars are uniquely qualified to speak on certain matters, therefore they must speak for themselves rather than allowing others to speak on their behalf. According to Delgado & Stefancic (2001), the CRT tenet called the "unique voice of color" (p. 9) posits that there are certain issues that CLD members are uniquely suited to speak about, and that is why their narratives are critical and meaningful. For many years, many of the dominant journals in education openly practiced tokenism when it came to publishing the works of CLD scholars, as evidenced by the emergence of a few CLD scholars whose works appeared in those journals. The "truth" should not be limited to a few privileged CLD scholars and special multicultural themes and issues. Indeed, today, CLD scholars recognize the danger of privileging the perspectives of only a few scholars.

For instance, Anderson (2004), a highly regarded critical race theorist critiqued the pathologization of African American culture—this culture has been blamed for the underachievement gap of African American children, a theory of oppositional culture that was advanced by the late John Ogbu (1990, 2002, 2003). As Ogbu (2002) theorized, African American learners are "probably discouraged from working hard to succeed in school by generations of collective experience" (pp. 22–23). Drawing heavily from Ogbu's initial works, McWhorter (2000) noted that the African American culture is the cause of the poor school performance by Black children. Though the scholarship of African American historians (see Cornelius, 1991) negates these claims, the lingering effect of Ogbu's works is undeniable. And therein lie the dangers of relying solely on perspectives expressed by a handful of CLD scholars without allowing dissenting CLD voices some equally visible venues to express their scholarly voices and engage their peers in a scholarly exchange.

Granting agencies can contribute to the presence of CLD scholars in major journals. Research conducted through funding helps to provide the content for redefining and creating novel paradigms and practices. As a result, CLD scholars must write grant proposals that focus on CLD children and youth, especially those with disabilities and/or gifts and talents. The results of these grant projects can lead to the dissemination of needed information to promote more positive student outcomes. For some CLD scholars, publishing represents the traditional value of giving back and elevating the community, in particular its youth—the future generation. Concomitant with creating appropriate alternative models, CLD scholars have the challenge of rebutting biased and inaccurate research about CLD populations (see Obiakor & Algozzine, 2007). In other words, CLD scholars have to operate from both offensive and defensive perspectives (e.g., creating, redefining, and rebutting inaccuracies) by focusing on "what is and what is not" (Hine, 1996; Hooks & West, 1991; Littleton, 1995). Littleton noted that defensive publishing consumes a large amount of time, yet it must be done, but not at the expense of creating and defining positive appropriate models and practices to influence service delivery for CLD learners. For CLD scholars, balance is a key to enhanced performance.

Advancing Career Opportunities Through Self-Determination

Professionals in higher education are well acquainted with "publish or perish" policies and practices. Publishing plays a decisive role in hiring, promoting, and tenure processes (Obiakor, 2008b). Where the work is published is important; works published in major journals are generally awarded more credit (Garrett & McLoughlin, 1995). A critically important question for CLD scholars in academia is: Who decides which journals are "major journals"? Is every journal that is touted to be a major journal truly so because it publishes scholarship that is indeed of the highest quality, or are major journals major because certain scholars have easy access to them? Understanding the power of words (e.g., naming a journal as a "major journal") is critical for educators (Obiakor, Smith, & Sapp, 2007). Some years ago, Scheurich (1993), a CRT scholar, argued that the longer one group is dominant, the more effectively "the styles of thinking, acting, speaking, and behaving of the dominant group...become the socially correct or privileged ways of thinking, acting, speaking, and behaving" (p. 7). He added

> The ways of the dominant group become universalized as measure of merit, hiring criteria, grading standards, predictors of success, correct grammar, appropriate behavior, and so forth, all of which are said to be distributed as differences in individual effort, ability, or intelligence. Membership in a social group and group-related, inequitable distribution of resources and power thus disappear under the guise of individualism. (p. 7)

Understanding the politics of tenure and promotion and the value placed upon publications that have appeared in certain journals is critical to the success of CLD scholars, particularly in research-heavy institutions. Further, understanding the insidious nature of discriminatory acts directed to them in regard to their scholarship, hiring, tenure, and promotion will equip CLD scholars with the necessary savvy to succeed despite the odds. Empirical evidence demonstrates that whether it is in hiring, tenure, or promotion, the credentials of CLD scholars are subjected to valuative filters that discredit them by questioning the rigor of the journals where their works are published, the quality of their education, or if the degree is received from a CLD institution under the mentorship of an unfamiliar CLD scholar (suggesting that the scholar under review might be interested in working on multicultural issues Sagaria, 2002). Although we have emphasized the importance of CLD scholars taking on multicultural issues in their scholarship, we do not want to appear to suggest that CLD scholarship ought to be essentialized to issues surrounding populations from CLD groups. Rather, we encourage CLD scholars to take on scholarship roles that are broadly conceived and far-reaching, but to not allow themselves to be tripped into colluding with disseminating information that is ruinous to the education of children from CLD backgrounds.

Clearly, the publishing process can present difficulties to many faculty members in colleges and universities (Glatthorn, 2002). Some of these difficulties can be particularly painful for new CLD faculty trying to adjust to their environmental milieu. When difficulties are externally induced (e.g., trying to urge CLD scholars to select nonmulticulturally related research themes in order to be accepted and promoted), the individual scholar, the special education field, and, more important, CLD children and youth (exceptional or not) become losers. On the other hand, when difficulties are self-induced (e.g., fear of rejection of manuscripts), everyone loses. Factors that serve to promote an increase in CLD scholars' publishing in major journals include (a) receptive editorial boards, (b) adequate representation of CLD scholars on editorial boards, (c) peer reviewers who possess appropriate levels of awareness and knowledge in multicultural issues, (d) sufficient time to think and write, (e) supportive mentoring systems, and (f) productive professionals providing a continuing stream of quality scholarship (Hooks & West, 1991; Littleton, 1995; Obiakor, 2008b; Spooner, Algozzine, Thurlow, Obiakor, & Heller, 1997).

Exercising Academic Freedom

Institutions of higher learning, like the society in which they exist, can sometimes be less receptive of issues related to cultural and linguistic differences. This lack of attention can manifest itself in low student ratings of CLD (Fouad & Carter, 1992) faculty and staff in teaching and stereotypic regard for scholarship and service (Erickson & Rodriguez, 1999). Bell (1985, 1992) highlighted many of these racially unjustified activities. As a result, the only redemption for a CLD professor is to write. Furthermore, writing acts as both therapy and opportunity opener. If the teaching load is heavy and much time is spent serving on committees as a "minority" figurehead, professional advancement will be very difficult (Ford, Broadway, Li, Queener, & Wallace, 2003). There is a danger in the CLD scholar's refusal to serve unnecessarily on committees with little recognition granted in tenure and promotion decisions. The American Psychological Association (APA, 1992) found rejecting committee appointments to be most costly to women and CLD faculty, especially when they are viewed as uncooperative and lazy.

CLD professors must be careful not to allow themselves to be set up for failure; writing is a big part of professional development and advancement. Even when they know they are being used by their institution, they need to be preparing themselves at all times for advancement and movement. Writing provides them with the freedom to have opportunities and make choices, especially as they (a) discover what they know, (b) advance their careers, (c) know the satisfaction that comes from making a difference in the lives of children and youth, and (d) become more effective in their roles (Glatthorn, 2002). To a large measure, writing involves personal actions that frequently lead to self-satisfaction and self-confidence. As Henson (1995) succinctly put it,

> Writing is an empowering activity. Many individuals enjoy the power they derive from writing and the power derived from subsequent publications. For example, professors enjoy the respect that they get from colleagues and students when their articles and books are used in classes....Perhaps the most meaningful empowerment is internal. Having a manuscript accepted for publication is evidence of your power; just knowing that your article has been approved by a national panel of experts in your field reassures you that you are on the cutting edge. (pp. 3-4)

LESSONS FROM EXPERIENCE: BEYOND MYTHS

In almost all areas of study, there appears to be invisibility of CLD voices. For instance, multicultural special education is a new phenomenon, and there is a dearth of works in this important area of education. According to Golnick and Chinn (1990), "throughout U.S. history, racial identification has been used by policy makers and much of the population to classify groups of people as inferior or superior to another racial group" (p. 85). This historical misclassification has led to racial stereotypes, labels, discrimination, exclusion, and illusionary conclusions. Today, because of this historical misclassification, scholars and educators of CLD backgrounds are forced to remain vigilant in their search for and dissemination of the "truth." As a result, voices that have been invisible in the literature are becoming not only visible, but also multiple and loud. Obiakor (2008a) and Pedersen (1991) agreed that this enthusiasm has elevated multiculturalism as an inevitable force worthy of complementing major theoretical frameworks such as humanism, behaviorism, and cognitive learning theory. This enthusiasm has produced scholarly writings that have attempted to equalize the negative effects of historical writings. Unfortunately, the real impact of such scholarly efforts is yet to be felt in special education. For children and youth with exceptionalities (and their families), the limited inclusion of research and writings by CLD scholars remains problematic. In addition, CLD scholars have been somehow ineffective in dealing with traditional exclusionary practices in their scholarly writings. For instance, deciding not to write because of rejection or other exclusionary policies appears counterproductive and self-defeating. This decision, in our opinion, is like accepting defeat before the war even begins.

To fully discuss divergent perspectives about writing in scholarly publications, we share the experiences we have garnered from our writing activities. These perspectives are based on (a) historical burdens of exclusion, (b) the Council for Exceptional Children's (CEC) current efforts, (c) mentoring opportunities, (d) editorial experiences, (e) avoidance attitudes, and (f) constraints of time and location.

Historical Burdens of Exclusion

There are historical burdens that CLD people continue to endure in mainstream society. These encumbrances have far-reaching effects on how they view opportunities and choices in education (Obiakor, 1993, 2008b). Ford, Bessent-Byrd, and Misaka (1997) researched written records and consulted with several elders in the field of special education to clarify and validate their findings regarding the contributions of CLD professionals. In terms of scholarly publications, their investigation concluded that CLD professional writings were limited in special education journals and other publications. They did, however, discover a few multicultural proceedings, sporadic issues of major CEC journals, and a couple of books targeted to address CLD issues in special education. Additionally, they found inconsistent inclusion of writings by CLD scholars within the major CEC journals about issues regarding CLD individuals with disabilities and/or gifts and talents.

Historically, culturally focused research and topics addressed by many CLD scholars tend not to receive the same level of acceptance as legitimate and quality research as nonculturally oriented topics (Ford et al., 1997; Hine, 1996; Hooks & West, 1991; Littleton, 1995; Spooner et al., 1997). Even the most privileged and prolific CLD "elder" and "more recent" scholars have their stories of frustration regarding acceptance and publishing of their work. Of course, frustration with the publication process is not the exclusive domain of CLD scholars. In this regard, two critical questions deserve some attention: Must one prove his/her scholarship and acceptance by writing about general issues without focusing on those having the most impact on youth from CLD backgrounds and their families? Must one's work on any topic be written in a conservative, status quo tone to be accepted by the editorial board of major journals?

The review process for publication typically uses a blind review of peer experts to evaluate the quality of the work. An essential concern within this process is reviewers' expertise on CLD issues. The literature continues to reveal the inadequate preparation of special education personnel to provide effective services for children and youth from CLD backgrounds (Ford et al., 1997; Obiakor, 2007, 2008a; Obiakor & Beachum, 2005; Obiakor et al., 2002). Several factors contribute to this issue, one being the lack of expertise by teacher educators themselves. Teacher educators comprise the largest percentage of most expert peer reviewers. Though these peer reviewers may be experts in special education, they may not be knowledgeable about genuine multicultural general and special education issues. Interestingly, the argument of reviewer expertise also recently surfaced when "qualitative" researchers perceived their work as less likely to be published in "quantitative" journals (Obiakor, 2008b).

Although we have witnessed some increase in CLD scholars' presence on editorial boards or as guest reviewers of major educational journals, these representations remain limited. An argument often used in defense of limited acceptance of CLD works within prestigious publications is that alternate culturally oriented publication outlets are available for these scholars (Obiakor, 2008b). This line of argument appears enticing, but it shifts responsibility and limits the literary mechanisms available to put forth research findings that can be used to influence policy decision making. Another issue surrounding peer expertise that needs attention is the valuing of the expertise of CLD scholars as peer reviewers. For example, although we have been involved in many projects as reviewers, we have sometimes been asked in a rather belittling manner to defend our expertise. We do not feel that other leaders in general and special education are forced to authenticate their expertise the way CLD scholars are implicitly forced to do. To really reduce these inconsistencies and historical burdens of exclusion, it is imperative that CLD persons think about writing as a contribution to history (see Tip 3.1).

TIP
3.1
Think about writing to create truths and reduce inconsistencies. Write to contribute to the future and to overcome the historical burdens of exclusion that sometimes characterized the past.

CEC's Current Efforts

Of late, there have been efforts by different professional organizations to be inclusive at all levels. For instance, CEC, the major organization that deals with the well-being of people with exceptionalities, recognizes that for inclusion to be successful there must be inclusion at the classroom, school, and community levels. More CLD scholars than before are on editorial boards of major CEC journals. Representatives of these major journals have consistently held national workshops to encourage CLD professionals to publish. Unfortunately, very few CLD persons take advantage of these sessions. At its annual conventions, CEC has continued to support more strand presentations of serious thinking and scholarship on multicultural special education. In addition, there have been multicultural summits to encourage a meeting of the minds and reveal critical issues facing multicultural persons in special education. These issues tend to be old and new—they highlight topics that attract major publication outlets (Algozzine, Obiakor, & Boston, 1998).

The establishment of the Division for Culturally and Linguistically Diverse Exceptional Learners (DDEL) by CEC many years ago provided an added boost in bringing to the forefront issues related to multicultural special education. DDEL publishes *Multiple Voices for Ethnically Diverse Exceptional Learners* (*Multiple Voices*), a refereed journal that addresses paradigms, research, policies, and daily school practices to reduce inequities in educational opportunities for CLD individuals with disabilities and/or gifts and talents. Two of the authors of this chapter have served as editors for *Multiple Voices;* at CEC's national level, there is more networking among CLD scholars. This networking milieu has provided mentoring opportunities for neophytes in the scholarly arena and some scholarly publications have resulted from these endeavors (see Tip 3.2). Two questions continue to be critical at this juncture. How can CLD members maximize the benefits of CEC's efforts? Similarly, how can CEC maximize the talents of its CLD members?

TIP
3.2

Take advantage of CEC's current efforts.
These efforts include summits and symposia highlighting topics that attract major publication outlets. Put together a manuscript or series of papers and actively seek publication sources. If the past has been unkind, let the future be better.

Mentoring Opportunities

Experiences in mentoring CLD scholars and educators tell us that writing myths can be debunked. We have been successful in mentoring CLD and international faculty who are repeatedly disenfranchised and invisible in teacher education. We agree with Henson's (1995) notion that "good writers are self-made, not born" (p. 24). We also agree that "barriers that impede the success of ethnic minority faculty in professional writing can be overcome" (Spooner et al., 1997, p. 14). Mentoring and networking provide ample opportunities for writing impediments to be removed. Obiakor (1997) observed that such a networking milieu provides multidimensional opportunities for experienced CLD scholars to mentor inexperienced ones. Many of the myths associated with scholarly writing could be easily addressed with appropriate mentoring, collaboration, and partnership (see Obiakor, 2008b). Mentoring fails when collaboration, consultation, and cooperation fail. Henson confirmed that "when personalities are compatible, collaborating can bring out the best in all. Each partner stimulates the other. The unique expertise of each writer complements that of the other. For academics who are required to publish, collaborating can accelerate the role of publishing of all partners" (p. 129). *Collaboration* and *partnership* in this instance mean shared responsibility toward mutual goals— they do not mean having another person do a greater portion of the job. They mean taking pride in your work through continuous communication as professionals. Obviously, people cannot collaborate when one is the "victim" and the other is the "victimizer" or when one is the "victim" and the other is the "savior." In this regard, CLD scholars must take advantage of mentoring opportunities (see Tip 3.3). They must also understand very early that whatever they put out is a reflection of them whether they like it or not (Algozzine et al., 1998; Obiakor, 2008b; Obiakor, Lomotey, & Rueda, 1997).

TIP
3.3

Discover a writing mentor.
As a mentee, demonstrate the willingness to learn. Do not be a victim or a victimizer. Contribute first with ideas and later with actions. Learn quickly and try to give more than you take.

Alexander-Floyd (2004) reiterated a critical dimension to consider in mentoring, that is, "learning the rules of engagement" (p. 66; see Tip 3.4). Rules and expectations for tenure are seldom clearly articulated in quantifiable terms across many institutions, colleges, or departments. This can be a real frustration for junior faculty who want to know precisely what is expected of them in order to make adequate progress to tenure. It is important to learn what those expectations are and how they are articulated in the tripartite roles of teaching, research, and service. In other words, we must learn how to read the politics of tenure and promotion very early. Additionally, we must balance expectations and demands of our work with developing resiliency through taking time to build a community of support to stave off loneliness and chilly institutional climate that often dogs those in out-of-way places.

TIP
3.4

Learn the rules of engagement.
Learn what the expectations are for tenure and promotion and how they are articulated in the tripartite roles of teaching, research, and service.

Editorial Experiences

Our experiences in serving as editors and editorial board members of scholarly journals have revealed that writing myths deserve debunking (Henson, 1995;

Obiakor, 2008b; Spooner et al., 1997). Henson identified these myths to include statements such as (a) I'm not sure I have what it takes, (b) I don't have time to write, (c) the editors will reject my manuscript because my name is not familiar to them, and (d) in my field there are few opportunities to publish. According to Spooner et al., "these myths can be dangerous to writers from ethnic minority backgrounds because they have broad self-concept and productivity implications. Writing is hard work, and perceptions that detract from our willingness to do it just make it more difficult" (p. 14). We believe in the old saying, "it ain't over 'til it's over." Our experiences have shown that many CLD writers take rejection too literally—they internalize rejection instead of looking at it as a way to better their works. Our own success in scholarly writing is based on our willingness to revise and resubmit our manuscripts. We acknowledge that race, color, and tribalization matter in all societal activities in the United States (Obiakor, 2008a; West, 1993); however, negative presumptions about publications pose serious challenges for CLD scholars. These presumptions tend to perpetuate the "victim" mentality which in itself hampers scholarly production and increases the blindness on human differences. We cannot in good faith deny the tremendous support that many of our non-CLD colleagues have given to us. Our experiences have also revealed that many of these same individuals are quite knowledgeable on issues related to CLD learners with exceptionalities (Obiakor & Ford, 1998).

TIP
3.5

Do not take editorial rejection too literally.
Take advantage of the free advice often provided in manuscript reviews. Revise and resubmit rejected manuscripts to the same source or other publication outlets. When frustrated, seek more advice from a mentor.

We cannot assume that all editorial rejections are based on racism or discrimination. A rejected article might be a good article that needs to be revised and resubmitted to either the same publication or another publication (see Tip 3.5). The presumption that you have to know somebody to publish is somehow wrong. Rather, when you write consistently, you are known. Consider this analogy. When a business produces quality products, many customers buy from it and it becomes popular and widely known. Before long, this business builds its own clientele and makes more profit than its competitors. A consistent writer is no different. When you do quality work, people will respect and reference it in their own works even when they disagree with you. Before long, you gain a credible national and international reputation, begin to serve on editorial boards of publications, and enjoy invitations to submit your works for publications in myriad outlets (Algozzine et al., 1998; Obiakor, 2008b; Obiakor & Ford, 1998).

Avoidance Attitudes

Tip
3.6

Be consistent.
Do not allow frustration to lead you into avoidance. Treat a letter of rejection as an opportunity to respond rather than a mandate to issue a death knell to a paper or as a reason to gripe and complain or become a victim.

When we think about our pains, trials, and tribulations in writing, giving up, giving in, or avoidance sometimes cross our minds. Our question continues to be: If we do not write, who will rectify the historical falsities and inconsistencies about us in the educational literature? This is a serious challenge to CLD scholars. Our experiences have revealed that avoidance attitudes create more problems and more stereotypes for CLD members in the scholarly arena. We must be consistent and persistent in telling our stories in writing in spite of our frustrations (see Tip 3.6). Spooner et al. (1997) wrote

- Because we all have stories to tell, we all have what it takes to be good writers. We must be self-motivated and self-empowered to write.
- We make time for whatever we like to do. We cannot dismiss the inconsistencies in our history unless we make time to write.
- There are many issues confronting us. These issues are worth writing about.
- Everyone's manuscript can be rejected. No one is immune from rejection. Rejection of a person's manuscript does not in any way mean rejection of that person.
- We improve our vocabulary and writing skills by writing. Remember, writers are self-made, not born.
- There are many opportunities for people from diverse cultural and linguistic backgrounds. Today, almost all professional conferences and publications focus on issues facing these groups. Because our demographics are changing, these issues cannot be swept under the rug.
- We must enjoy the power that writing brings. To decry tokenism, we must enjoy the power associated with publication of books, monographs, articles, and other forms of writing. We cannot continue to be victims. We must define ourselves through our works.
- We must collaborate, consult, and cooperate with people. Writing enhances teamwork and teamwork enhances writing. Individuals in different institutions can have similar interests and different perspectives that enrich written products.
- Our freedoms are incomplete unless we express them. An important medium for such expression is writing. (pp. 14-15)

Constraints of Time and Location

Lack of time and time management are frequently cited as primary stumbling blocks to publishing (Algozzine et al., 1998; Cook, 2007; Hine, 1996; Obiakor, 2008b; Spooner et al., 1997). Scholars in higher education have to acclimate themselves to the general barriers and stress of managing time to write (Glatthorn, 2002). Common complaints include too many committees, large numbers of advisees, and heavy teaching loads. In addition to the demands on most professionals, many CLD faculty and staff in predominately White colleges and universities are often pulled in several other directions: (a) being called upon by departments to serve on committees needing departmental representation by CLD faculty; (b) serving as unofficial advisors, role models, and mentors for ethnic minority undergraduate and graduate students; and (c) responding to demands for participation from social or civic organizations (e.g., churches, mosques, and synagogues) within local communities (Hine).

TIP
3.7
Prioritize obligations.
Know what obligations are really important to you and fulfill them regardless of the cost to you.

Demographic changes in academia have ushered in CLD faculty, and also those who are younger, female, and with young children. The disparate nature of responsibilities that some of the CLD scholars whose identities are located at the intersection of race, age, gender, and motherhood are faced with challenges that are uniquely different from those who have traditionally occupied faculty roles. The challenges posed by the multidimensional and sometimes oppositional roles are many and varied. Tenured women with young children are sometimes encouraged to remain at the associate level and have to work really hard to shatter "the mommy ceiling" (Mutua, in press). However, the challenges can be distilled to *time*. The issue for this unique group is not merely time management; it is balancing the competing demands for time that come about as a result of these multifaceted roles. The need to prioritize obligations (White & Meendering, 2008) and rank order them by importance becomes a matter of urgency. A CLD female faculty with young children and a growing family quickly recognizes how inconsequentially academia treats young children. Therefore, people must be very clear in their mind what is really important and accord it top priority regardless of the compromises they have to make in some other endeavors (see Tip 3.7).

> *Manage your time.*
>
> Tip
> **3.8**   If you are in any location, collaborate and consult with others of similar scholarly interests. Actively seek collegial relations; don't wait for them to knock on your door.

Non-CLD professionals adjusting to new geographic locations may experience feelings of loneliness and isolation. However, for CLD professionals, in particular females, these feelings may be more frustrating, especially in small, predominantly White college towns (Hine, 1996). These feelings combined with other responsibilities (e.g., family and church) may limit energy and time for research and publishing. Thus, it becomes necessary to be aware of and embrace effective techniques to enhance collaboration and consultation in publishing. From our perspective, the best solution is to network, collaborate, and consult with other colleagues who have similar scholarly interests. Consistency in time management is the key (see Tip 3.8).

> *Learn when to say "no."*
>
> Tip
> **3.9**   If taking on a particular service responsibility takes away from your research time, then decline it. In many research-oriented institutions, service will not grant you favorable tenure reviews; publishing will.

The issue of time has many critical elements that can trip unsuspecting junior CLD faculty. As stated earlier, CLD faculty, particularly those in predominantly White institutions, often find themselves constantly called upon to serve on committees and perform other "nonrewarded" service activities. Refusal to serve as stated often leads to being branded lazy, uncooperative, and a nonteam player (APA, 1992). However, junior faculty members must learn to say "no" early when such responsibilities interfere with their research time (Alexander-Floyd, 2004). It is important to serve your department, college, and the university at large as well as having other important and visible academic citizenship activities outside the institution. However, you should be clear in your mind where the line is in the sand that demarcates enough and too much time on service—and know when you cross it and how not to cross it (see Tip 3.9).

TIPS FOR SUCCESS IN EXPRESSING CLD SCHOLARLY VOICES

TIP **3.10**	*Write, write, and write some more!* Enjoy what you do; keep your eyes on the prize; and add depth, perspective, and weight to multiple voices. Do not expect the world to provide a living. Look for opportunities and turn them into evidence of competence, credibility, and creation.

CLD scholars cannot afford to be silent, and our profession cannot afford to leave their voices unheard. The reasons to write go beyond the usual writing for pleasure or promotion. When CLD members write, they create truths and respond to inaccuracies. We enjoy the trials and tribulations of writing and we continue to learn a lot about writing by writing (see Tip 3.10). Based on our experiences, we strongly believe in maximizing the potential for writing in scholarly publications. We also believe like Glatthorn (2002) that "writing that is not published is like a tree that falls in the forest with no one there to hear" (p. 4). As a result, CLD members of the academy must

- Participate in workshops, seminars, and panels that lead to research opportunities.
- Select an area of study that is personally or professionally meaningful and develop a research theme.
- Present at national conferences and submit work to ERIC Clearinghouses.
- Become a member of or create a network of publishing professionals.
- Submit manuscripts to both traditional and culturally oriented special education publications.
- Submit manuscripts to general and mainstream education journals and other publication outlets.
- Write in order to learn how to write.
- Reject historical burdens of exclusion.
- Revise a rejected manuscript and resubmit it.
- Ask to serve on editorial boards.
- Manage time effectively.
- Become a mentor and mentee depending on experience, expertise, and need.
- Write some more even when known in the field— this is when ideas might be getting the attention they deserve in the literature.
- Be persistent and consistent about writing in scholarly publications.
- Enjoy what they do.

PERSPECTIVE

In this era of the devolution of affirmative action in institutions of higher education (IHEs) across the country (*Gratz V. Bollinger,* 2003; *Grutter v. Bollinger,* 2003), race is no longer a compelling interest of IHEs. Therefore, there are fewer equity avenues for hiring CLD scholars. For those of us already in the academy, the need to speak or write is not only more necessary, but critically urgent. During these times, we cannot afford the luxury of silence or mediocrity. Bell's (1980) principle of interest convergence—"the interest for Blacks in achieving racial equality will be accommodated only when it converges with the interests of Whites" (p. 523)—reminds us that our voices in the academy may well be accommodated at this time. Within many fields, the academy is undergoing a cathartic self-appraisal, and therefore wants to appear to be inclusive of voices previously excluded in academic discourse. As CLD scholars choose to write, they must know not only their subjects but their audience and outlets. Accordingly, they must know that the selection of certain outlets comes with high costs in hiring, tenure, and promotion. So, for junior faculty, the careful selection of outlets is critically important. Another word of caution especially for junior faculty is to be aware that pursuit of academic freedom can be costly, particularly in mistakes where one is attempting to connect research and service (White & Meendering, 2008). Earlier, Finley (2000) demonstrated the peril to tenure for junior faculty whose academic freedoms, she argued, "are abridged during their pre-appointment" (p. 7). Senior faculty who are not hampered by looming terror of perishing from tenure and promotion review, must write without apology. CLD faculty must tell their own story in their own words, knowing that no one can tell their story better than they can (Mutua & Swadener, 2004; Swadener & Mutua, 2008).

This chapter has addressed reasons for CLD voices to be heard in the literature. We used personal experiences to share our ideas about writing for publication without fear. Because we agree race, color, and tribalization continue to matter today in general and special education programs, CLD scholars and educators have the obligation to debunk existing negative stereotypes that lead to illusionary conclusions. We understand the barriers that hamper scholarly publications of CLD persons exist, but we also know from experience that these barriers can be overcome. To deal with them, we must understand the intricacies of writing for publication (e.g., to be a good writer, one must write). Our collective experiences tell us that we cannot afford to be victims of our external or internal circumstances. We must tell our stories in writing to reduce racist presumptions and historical inconsistencies in the literature. Through writing, we are bound to create truths, equalize negative traditional writings, build scholarly reputations, advance professionally, and exercise our academic freedom. The solution is the same for everyone: Be known by what you do, not by reasons you can find to justify not performing.

REFERENCES

Alexander-Floyd, N. G. (2004). The seven habits of highly successful black junior faculty. *Black Issues in Higher Education, 21*(10), 66.

Algozzine, B., Obiakor, F. E., & Boston, J. M. (1998). *Publish and flourish: A guide for writing in education.* Arlington, VA: Council for Exceptional Children.

American Psychological Association. (1992). *Survival guide to academia for women and ethnic minorities.* Washington, DC: Author.

Anderson, J. D. (2004). Crosses to bear and promises to keep: The jubilee anniversary of *Brown v. Board of Education. Urban Education, 39,* 359-373.

Barnet, S., & Bedau, H. (1989). *Current issues and enduring questions: A guide to critical thinking and argument, with readings.* Boston: Bedford/St. Martin's.

Bell, D. (1980). *Brown v. Board of Education* and the interest convergence dilemma. *Harvard Law Review, 93,* 518-533.

Bell, D. (1985). *And we are not saved: The elusive quest for racial justice.* New York: Basic Books.

Bell, D. (1992). *Faces at the bottom of the well: The permanence of racism.* New York: Basic Books.

Cook, S. D. (2007). What new faculty women wish they'd known earlier. *Women in Higher Education, 15*(12), 1-2.

Cornelius, J. D. (1991). *When I can read my title clear: Literacy, slavery, and religion in the Antebellum South.* Columbia: University of South Carolina Press.

Delgado, R., & Stefancic, J. (2001). *Critical race theory: An introduction.* New York: New York University Press.

Erickson, C. D., & Rodriguez, E. R. (1999). Indiana Jane and the temples of doom: Recommendations for enhancing women and racial/ethnic faculty's success in academia. *Innovative Higher Education, 24,* 149-168.

Finley, S. (2000). Strangers in the academy: Beginning professors in pursuit of (academic) freedom. *Teacher Education Quarterly, 27,* 49-64.

Ford, B. A., Bessent-Byrd, H., & Misaka, J. (1997, April). *Contributions of culturally and linguistically diverse ethnic groups to changing paradigms in special education.* Paper presented at the International Convention of the Council for Exceptional Children, Salt Lake City, UT

Ford, B. A., Broadway, F., Li, H., Queener, J., & Wallace, J. (2003, October). *Multicultural praxis in teacher education: Promise and predicament.* Paper presented at the American Council on Education, Atlanta, GA.

Ford, B. A., Obiakor, F. E., & Patton, J. M. (1995). *Effective education of African American exceptional learners: New perspectives.* Austin, TX: PRO-ED.

Fouad, N. A., & Carter, R. T. (1992). Gender and racial issues for new counseling psychologists in academia. *The Counseling Psychologist, 20,* 123-140.

Garrett, J. E., & McLoughlin, J. A. (1995). A reference for judging the quality of publication in special education and related services journals. *Teacher Education and Special Education, 18,* 133-138.

Glatthorn, A. A. (2002). *Publish or perish: The educator's imperative.* Thousand Oaks, CA: Corwin Press.

Golnick, D. M., & Chinn, P. C. (1990). *Multicultural education in a pluralistic society* (3rd ed.). New York: Merrill.

Gratz v. Bollinger, 539 U.S. 244 (2003).

Grutter v. Bollinger, 539 U.S. 306 (2006).

Henson, K. T. (1995). *The art of writing for publication.* Needham Heights, MA: Allyn & Bacon.

Hine, D. C. (1996). *Speak truth to power: Black professional class in United States history.* Brooklyn, NY: Carlson.

Hooks, B., & West, C. (1991). *Insurgent black intellectual life.* Boston: South End Press.

Littleton, A. C. (1995). Research in education: Methodological and theoretical consideration. *Journal of Negro Education, 45,* 78-88.

McWhorter, J. H. (2000). *Losing the race: Self-sabotage in Black America.* New York: Free Press.

Mutua, K. (in press). Pedagogical accent in teacher education: Narrating self within/against pedigrees and stereotypes of race and national origin. In F. E. Obiakor, P. Grant & S. O. Obi (Eds.). *Voices of foreign-born African American Teacher Education*: Hauppauge, NY; Nova Science Publishers.

Mutua, N. K., & Swadener, B. B. (Eds.) (2004). *Decolonizing research in cross-cultural contexts: Critical personal narratives.* Albany, SUNY Press.

Obiakor, F. E. (1993). Opportunity and choice in higher education: Perspectives of African American scholars. *SAEOPP Journal: Journal of the Southeastern Association of Educational Opportunity Program Personnel, 12,* 31-44.

Obiakor, F. E. (1997). Networking: African American dilemma. *Special Educators News and Update, 2,* 2-6.

Obiakor, F. E. (1998). *Black at last.* In B. Algozzine, F. E. Obiakor, J. N. Boston (Eds.), *Publish and flourish: A guide for writing in education* (p. 11), Arlington, Va; Council for Exceptional Children.

Obiakor, F. E. (2007). *Multicultural special education: Culturally responsive teaching.* Upper Saddle River, NJ: Pearson Merrill Prentice Hall.

Obiakor, F. E. (2008a). *The eight-step approach to multicultural teaching and learning* (3rd ed.). Dubuque, IA. Kendell/Hunt.

Obiakor, F. E. (2008b, April). *Understanding publication as the "egg and yolk of one's shell."* Position paper presented at the 2nd Annual College of Education Research Conference, Grambling State University, Grambling, LA.

Obiakor, F. E., & Algozzine, B. (2007). Executive editor's comments: Debunking perceptions that impede multicultural education. *Multicultural Learning and Teaching, 2*(1), ii.

Obiakor, F. E, & Beachum, F. E. (2005). *Urban education for the 21st century: Research, issues, and perspectives.* Springfield, IL: Charles C Thomas.

Obiakor, F. E., & Ford, B. A. (1998). Expressing diverse, minority scholar voices. In B. Algozzine, F. E. Obiakor, J. N. Boston (Eds.), *Publish and flourish: A guide for writing in education* (pp. 11-16). Arlington, VA: Council for Exceptional Children.

Obiakor, F. E., & Ford, B. A. (2002). *Creating successful learning environments for African American learners with exceptionalities.* Thousand Oaks, CA: Corwin Press.

Obiakor, F. E., Grant, P., & Dooley, E. (2002). *Educating all learners: Refocusing the comprehensive support model.* Springfield, IL: Charles C Thomas.

Obiakor, F. E., Lomotey, K., & Rueda, R. (1997, January). *Writing for publication.* Paper presented at the Multicultural Symposium of the Division for Culturally and Linguistically Diverse Exceptional Learners (DDEL), the Council for Exceptional Children, New Orleans, LA.

Obiakor, F. E., Smith, D. J., & Sapp, M. (2007). Understanding the power of words in multicultural education. *Multicultural Perspectives, 9,* 36-42.

Ogbu, J. U. (1990). Minority education in comparative perspective. *Journal of Negro Education, 59*(1), 45-47.

Ogbu, J. U. (2002, Winter). Black-America students and the academic achievement gap: What else you need to know. *Jounral of American Thought,* 9-33.

Ogbu, J. U. (2003). *Black American students in an affluent suburb: A study of academic engage.* Mahway, NJ: Lawrence Erlbaum.

Pedersen, P. B. (1991, September/October). Multiculturalism as a generic approach to counseling. *The Journal of Counseling and Development, 70,* 6-12.

Phillips, M. C. (1993). Tenure trap: Number of obstacles stand in way of tenure for women. *Black Issues in Higher Education, 21,* 42-43, 45.

Rogers, L. J., & Swadener, B. B. (1999). Reflections on the future work on anthropology and education: Reframing the field. *Anthropology and Education Quarterly, 30,* 436-440.

Sagaria, M.A.D. (2002). The exploratory model of filtering in administrative searches: Toward counter-hegemonic discourses. *The Journal of Higher Education, 73,* 677-710.

Scheurich, J. J. (1993). Toward a white discourse on white racism. *Educational Researcher, 22,* 5-10.

Spooner, F., Algozzine, B., Thurlow, M., Obiakor, F., & Heller, H. W. (1997). Ethnic minority scholars writing for professional publication: From myth to reality. *Multiple Voices, 2,* 12-20.

Swadener, E., & Mutua, K. (2008). Decolonizing performances: Deconstructing the global postcolonial. In N. Denzin, Y. Lincoln, & L. T. Smith. (Eds.), *Handbook of critical and indigenous methodologies.* Thousand Oaks, CA: Sage.

West, C. (1993). *Race matters.* New York: Vintage Books.

White, J., & Meendering, J. (2008). Four basic strategies for success in the early years of higher education. *The Delta Kappa Gamma Bulletin, 74*(3), 32-34.

4 Overcoming Challenges That Face New Writers

Mark B. Goor and
Thierry Kolpin

They can because they think they can.

~ Virgil

New faculty often believe they were thrown from the dock and that they are either going to sink or swim (Solem & Foote, 2006). Surveys of junior faculty (Austin, 2002; Hamilton, 1996; Renegar, 1993) reveal that most had no experience with publication during their doctoral programs to prepare them for this career requirement. These faculty members imagined when they began their new profession there would be pressure to publish, but certainly there would be the time and support to succeed in this endeavor. Instead, new faculty members find themselves overwhelmed with teaching and institutional responsibilities (Boice, 1993) while realizing at the same time that senior faculty have little intention of being their mentors (Renegar, 1993; Sorcinelli, 1994). The same institutions that advertise positions for assistant professors with strong evidence of potential for scholarly achievement, essentially defined as successful publishing, make little or no provisions for providing the time or developing the necessary skills. The culture expects self-initiative and heroic dedication.

In spite of this lack of preparation and support, many new faculty members succeed as writers. Why is that? Successful writers confront their apprehension about writing and fear of rejection. They identify multiple sources of issues and select ideas they care about deeply. They make the time to write and push past the blocks to productiveness. They cultivate their creativity and demonstrate willingness to contact editors and take criticism constructively. They enlist support of peers, senior faculty, and administrators. In addition, they edit their work ruthlessly and pay careful attention to guidelines and details of manuscript submission. Most of all, they enjoy the rewarding journey. This chapter addresses these areas and the following subsections discuss each in more detail.

CONFRONTING FEARS

To publish, new faculty members must confront writing anxiety. Most people have "writing apprehension" which centers primarily around locus of control (Rechtien & Dizinno, 1997). People with an internal locus of control are better at managing stress and anxiety (Treven & Potocan, 2005). In other words, the degree to which writers feel they have control over their own success determines their relative anxiety with the process. Henson (1987) recalled that successful writers say "I can and will succeed," while unsuccessful writers are consumed by the fear of rejection. Thus, as in most areas of competence and performance, attitude appears to distinguish successful from unsuccessful writers (Rau, 2007; see Tip 4.1) . Indeed, new faculty could benefit from a slight change of the current societal emphasis "Yes we can" to "Yes I can." The successful writer has confidence and determination, and apprehension is diminished when enjoyment replaces anxiety related to writing.

TIP
4.1

Attitude is not everything but it clearly matters in performing most skills.
Believing that writing is important, believing that competence in writing can be learned, and believing that you can write are convictions that shape powerful writers. Remember: Attitude is one characteristic that distinguishes successful writers from unsuccessful writers.

Seeking Topics

Successful writers know the current issues because they read (Westermann, 1994), attend conferences (Henson, 1987) and collaborate with schools (Paul, Duchnowski, & Danforth, 1993). Good writers are good readers (Westermann). They explore many potential sources for publishing, obtaining a sense of each journal's topic areas, audiences, variations in style and formats, as well as the importance of research to each. Writers attend conferences to identify current topics and to create professional networks (Henson, 1987, 2005a, 2005b). Themes of presentations at these professional meetings provide insights into subjects of contemporary interest, and presenters often discuss their current research. If young writers of similar interests have creative sparks ignited at a conference, they can talk to presenters about related research or writing ideas (see Tip 4.2).

Collaboration with schools provides a rich source of writing ideas (Burton & Greher, 2007). In a special issue of *Teacher Education and Special Education*, faculty members from the University of South Florida described how a commitment to collaborate with schools was creating a new vision of teacher education and research (Paul et al., 1993). Partnerships with educators and parents test educational theory, foster collaborative thinking, and stimulate new ideas for research and publication.

In addition, many new faculty members have dissertation research data that can be translated into articles. This is best done immediately as interest in dissertation topics often cools quickly. New professors are generally comfortable and knowledgeable on their dissertation topics. Dissertation research provides a bridge from the doctoral experience to faculty publication. Frequently dissertation topics contain enough research to result in multiple manuscript submissions, and can open the door to other areas of interest (Henson, 2005a, 2005b; Kamler, 2008).

TIP
4.2

Nobody knows everything and nothing lasts forever.
New ideas are everywhere. Find current topics by reviewing the work of your colleagues, attending conferences, and collaborating with other professionals.

Finding Passion

Reading, attending conferences, and collaborating may result in many ideas for publication, but it is vital to select a topic the writer cares about deeply (Clark, 1994; Neumann, 2006). Westermann (1994) suggested that authors should write about personal experiences that give power and color to their writing. Authors who participate and observe write with authenticity.

TIP
4.3

One of the marks of productive writers is the ability to convert passion into action.
An action becomes genuinely important when it springs from intrinsic motivation. Writing is hard work, and passion for the topic may be the only incentive that gets authors through difficult times.

Writing can be hard work, and passion for the topic may be the only motivation that gets authors through difficult times (Mayrath, 2008; see Tip 4.3) . Writers develop relationships with their topic and their manuscripts. As with all relationships, writers must learn to live through disappointments and frustrations by holding the vision for their work. Sometimes putting aside a project for a while, or seeking guidance to move past perceived blocks, is just as necessary as getting space or counseling is to the health of a human relationship.

Making Time

Top selling novelist Barbara Kingsolver contends there is no perfect time to write; there is only now (in Clark, 1994). Henson (2005b) recognized that many authors work best at a certain time of day; some write better first thing in the morning while others prefer late nights. Clark noted that artistic inspiration is overrated and recommended writing daily. If an author waits for the inspiration to write, the project may never get finished.

On the path to tenure, new faculty are often given moderate structure for course time, office hours, committee meetings, yet little is offered for writing and research. Boice (1993) observed that successful writers develop self-discipline and patience. Successful writers do not *have* the time to write, they *make* the time to write, scheduling writing like they schedule teaching, meetings, and appointments (see Tip 4.4). Too often, when writing time is conceptualized as a few stolen moments to get as much done as possible, writing projects and products languish or remain unfulfilled and unrealized.

TIP **4.4**	*The best way to lose time is to waste it.* Time is a great equalizer—nobody has too much of it. Successful writers do not *have* the time to write, they *make* the time to write. Learn to use time as a tool, not an excuse.

Pushing Past the Block

Newer faculty may work through perceived blocks by simply writing as one would in a blog, chat room, text messaging, or e-mail. Henson (1990) recommended writing fast to get it down, then adding, subtracting, and modifying later (see Tip 4.5). Some authors believe that their self-critical nature slows their progress; successful writers know that writing is like brainstorming and that editing follows (Boice, 1992; Henson, 2005a, 2005b).

Many authors set specific, realistic goals for each writing session (Hamilton, 1996). Clark (1994) suggested ending writing with an idea for what to do next. This reduces the anxiety of facing the blank page. Instead, the writer returns with motivation to start again. Westermann (1994) advised creating an outline for the draft. The outline helps to structure the task so that when the writer bogs down on one section, there are other sections to address. An outline also promotes an integrated whole in which there is a relationship between all sections of the writing. To this effect, the introduction should direct the manuscript toward a unifying theme that finds completion in the conclusion.

TIP
4.5

Pen, pencil, word processor, table, time, and inclination aside, few writers are always eager to write.
When a block occurs it sometimes helps to write thoughts rather than convictions, and phrases rather than sentences; it always helps to write them down fast, then add, subtract, and modify them later.

Cultivating Creativity

Writers have days when they do not feel particularly insightful, or they feel hopelessly uncreative (See Tip 4.6). Sternberg's (1997) research on intelligence led him to conclude that there are three types of intelligence that can be enhanced: creative, analytical, and practical. He offered hope for cultivating creative intelligence by suggesting that people (a) believe in themselves, (b) find what they love to do, (c) capitalize on their strengths, (d) learn the knowledge base but do not let it confine them, (e) tolerate ambiguity, (f) be willing to take sensible risks, (g) make mistakes and learn from them, (h) allow time to be creative, (i) maintain their sense of humor, (j) persevere in overcoming obstacles, (k) think long term and consider things in a larger context, and (l) ask for other ways to define and solve problems. Obviously no one can manifest all of these positive actions, but as we know from assets development, the more that can be embraced the greater the likelihood of success. Garrison Keillor echoes many of these ideas, adding, "be bold and thrust forward and have the courage to fail" (in Clark, 1994, p. 8).

One major component of writing and creativity includes taking care of self. With the stressors accompanying a new faculty position and pressures to publish, it is imperative that new writers are mindful of their physical and psychological needs. Some faculties have developed peer writing support groups to help lessen the stressors associated with new responsibilities (Tysick & Babb, 2006), while others profess the importance of engaging in activities completely outside of academia (Perlmutter, 2008). Regardless of how one chooses to manage stress, creativity can grow and flourishes from a healthy foundation.

> TIP
> **4.6**
> *A blank sheet of paper or a "new" word processing file can be an intimidating start to a creative writing project.*
> Be bold, thrust forward, and have the courage to learn something from failure and write on.

Dispelling the "Evil Editor" Myth

Many new writers have conjured an erroneous image of the rejecting editor who feels joy in ripping apart one's best work (See Tip 4.7). Henson's (1990) survey of refereed journals in education revealed that most editors welcome queries from potential authors. As a matter of fact, editors recommend authors write a letter asking if the topic would be of interest to the journal and readership. This letter should demonstrate knowledge of the journal with comments about the type of articles the inquiring author has read that indicate the readership might be interested. Based on personal experience as an editor, Natriello (1996) advised writing to editors but cautioned authors to be courteous even in the face of disappointment. Editors have their own frustrations with the review process. Their reviewers return manuscripts late, and editors often have to respond to complaints about critical feedback and rejection.

> TIP
> **4.7**
> *When working with editors, be open to criticism and learn from it.*
> Some people believe editors separate the wheat from the chaff and then publish the chaff. Most editors know the difficulty of writing and remember their personal reactions to rejection. Let them do their thing and be open to learning something.

Most editors know the difficulty of writing and remember their personal reactions to rejection. These editors are often good teachers and wise counselors (Henson, 1987, 2005; Nihalani, 2008). They have sound advice concerning how to organize and clarify writing so that it flows. Editors can suggest how to modify a manuscript to conform to their journal. Most beginners write too much. Editors can help to eliminate extra verbiage so that articles are succinct and powerful. Many writers lament not having heeded editors' advice (Clark, 1994). Excessive self-criticism is debilitating but insufficient self-criticism is the handmaiden of mediocrity.

Enlisting Support

Writing can be a lonely endeavor. Some writers prefer to work with others. "When it's good, it's very good"; co-authors may have complementary strengths and may be a source of emotional support. "But, when it's bad, it's awful"; many co-authors find they have incompatible concerns with timelines and commitment to specific tasks. Henson's (1987) advice for co-authors is to develop specific timelines and clarify responsibilities continuously. Co-authors can alternate taking the lead on projects to balance workloads.

Paul, Marfo, and Anderson (1996) described a powerful group structure called collaborative research groups (CRG), which are teams of faculty and doctoral students with shared interests in an area of applied research. The CRG process encourages comparisons of personal experiences and fosters reflection on long-held assumptions. In this instance, group members offer collegial support for completing research tasks and writing through a "writer's guild" at the University of Wisconsin-Milwaukee. As a result they implement training for group members in constructive review techniques and develop supportive group responses to common writing roadblocks (Padgett & Begun, 1996).

Even if an author does not write with others, good writers seek the advice of others (see Tip 4.8). Hamilton (1996) recommended finding a mentor successful in publishing. Many senior faculty are honored by the acknowledgment of their talent and the request for their guidance. Boice (1993) indicated that nothing ensures a strong start in successful publication more than mentors and support networks. Some universities are using peer mentoring support networks to assist new faculty with the tenure and promotion process, especially with regards to writing (Lewallen, Crane, Letvak, Jones, & Hu, 2003). At the very least, successful writers ask others to read their work, and they accept suggestions as necessary refinement in the development of better manuscripts (Fine, 1988).

New writers must be forthright in asking for help from deans and department chairs. Beginning faculty members should clarify the university expectation for research and publication to develop their personal goals. When setting goals for writing, new faculty members should consider the full range of their responsibilities while at the same time creating a vision for their future careers (which may involve life at another university with different expectations). Based on this information, new faculty members might discuss long-term plans and how the resources of the university could be used to support them. This initiative makes a clear statement of new faculty members' awareness and commitment as well as the justifiable belief that there should be support throughout the process. This initiative may spur administrators to channel available resources that might have been used for other purposes.

> **TIP 4.8**
>
> *Sometimes advice is what we ask for when we already know an answer but wish we didn't.*
>
> Sometimes we seek approval from others for a course already charted. The trick is to use advice to generate light more than heat.

Editing Ruthlessly

For many writers, first drafts are often mediocre at best (Westermann, 1994). Clark (1994) cautioned that if you fall in love with a first draft, you greatly enhance the possibilities of never getting it published. Garrison Keillor (in Clark, 1994) wrote, "When in doubt, read it out loud...it helps you know what is bad so you can eliminate it or else use a pseudonym" (p. 3). Westermann imagined his audience when reading aloud and made notes about what they would not like or what needed to be clarified.

Successful writers ask colleagues, family, friends, and/or partners with good editing skills to inspect manuscripts for errors. Sometimes an editor's decision to reject rather than revise is based on the presence of multiple errors giving the impression of carelessness. In addition, editors look for manuscripts with good overall organization that ease the work of the reader. Good writers organize content into clear paragraphs and use subheadings (See Tip 4.9).

> **TIP 4.9**
>
> *Editing may seem like fighting with your own words, but good writers know that writing demands repair.*
>
> Be careful not to be too hard and lose the benefit. Remember that it is harder to write a short letter than a long one, and the work is in editing.

Submitting Effectively

Writers seeking to publish must get to know the kind of work a journal publishes (see Tip 4.10), and attempt to match the style of writing to the journal (Carriuolo, Boylan, Simpson, Bader, & Calderwood, 2007). There are several ways to identify the style of a journal. When reading what has been published, one can examine articles to determine their length, organization, and special features, such as case studies or recommendations for practice. In addition, editors periodically write commentary and statements of interest in the front of the journal.

In terms of the importance of research, readers can assess whether specific journals (a) merely demonstrate an awareness of research in the field, (b) explain the application of research to practice, or (c) actually describe a specific research project. It may be tempting for new authors to brazenly challenge the status quo. This approach risks rejection. Writers may be more successful if they acknowledge tradition and then pose thoughtful questions based on new data.

All journals publish directions for submissions, including format, number of copies, and additional requirements. It surprises editors how many manuscripts are submitted that appear as if the contributing authors have ignored guidelines. Successful writers study directions for submission and follow them explicitly. If a manuscript is returned for revision, successful authors revise. A conversation among editors (Natriello, 1996) revealed that only half of manuscripts returned for revision were resubmitted. Revised manuscripts have a greater chance of publication than first-time submissions. It is important to read editorial suggestions several times to understand fully what the editor and reviewers are seeking. Letters from editors generally indicate which suggestions are critical and which are optional. When returning revised manuscripts, successful writers include letters detailing how concerns were addressed in the revisions. If the writer disagrees with an editorial question or comment, then the rationale should be included as well. This letter, with explanation and rationale, communicates to the editor that the suggestions were valued and carefully considered.

TIP
4.10

Understand that every journal is different.
A simple way to ensure failure is to submit a manuscript without considering the purpose, audience, history, content, and style of the journal being considered as the publication source. Successful authors in every area of writing know the kind of work selected sources publish, and they try to cater in every way possible to the direction this information provides to their own work.

PERSPECTIVE

We end our chapter with an interesting lesson from the personal journey of a college professor. As a new faculty member, Dr. G knew he had to publish. When his department chair asked what topic or research he might write about, he felt like he was looking his worst fear right in the face. He was teaching four new classes and settling his family into a new habitat; plus, it seemed someone always needed him "desperately" whenever he was not in his office. Yet, if he was going to succeed at publishing and at advancing his career, he realized he had to schedule at least two writing mornings a week at home.

Dr. G had an idea that intrigued him. As a doctoral student, he had participated in research with a faculty member (Morine-Dershimer, 1991). He and a colleague replicated the study in a middle school and submitted a description of the research to *TEACHING Exceptional Children*. Several months later, they received positive feedback on the idea, but the manuscript needed to be completely revised to appeal to the journal's audience. They revised the article, and it was accepted.

Applying a similar research idea to college students, Dr. G generated another manuscript for a research journal in psychology. Months later, the feedback arrived with a three-page rejection letter questioning their method and commenting on this writing. Dr. G threw the letter on the department chair's desk and demanded some kind of encouragement. The chair shared a brief history of his own rejections and acceptances. But, Dr. G was inconsolable and refused to reread the letter for a month. After cooling off, he and his colleague read the letter carefully and saw the wisdom in the comments. They responded to the editorial concerns and resubmitted the manuscript. This time the rejection letter was only two pages of questions and comments, stating that further revisions would probably not help the article conform to the journal. They revised the manuscript based on some final comments of that editor and submitted the article to another journal. The editor of this journal responded enthusiastically, accepting the manuscript with minor revisions, and praising its unique conceptualization, well-written style, and appropriateness for the journal.

Dr. G took every rejection personally, but he had a passion for sharing his ideas, and he was determined to learn how to write better. Years later, as associate editor of two journals and reviewer for several others, he came to know editors personally and find them to be hard-working, caring professionals. He also realizes the importance of the support offered him at the beginning of his career. There were a few colleagues who were always willing to listen, provide encouragement, and critique ideas. In addition, his most notable publications were co-authored. Although co-authoring was rarely simple, the synergism consistently resulted in superior manuscripts. In the end, Dr. G now knows that writing for publication tests self-confidence every step of the way, yet he knows of no more effective process to clarify his thoughts and share his ideas with other educators. Finally, writing continues to be a fascinating, ever-unfolding journey.

REFERENCES

Austin, A. (2002). Preparing the next generation of faculty: Graduate school as socialization to the academic career. *Journal of Higher Education, 73,* 94-122.

Boice, R. (1992). *The new faculty member.* San Francisco: Jossey-Bass.

Boice, R. (1993). Early turning points in professional careers of women and minorities. *New Directions for Teaching and Learning, 53,* 71-79.

Burton, S. L., & Greher, G. R. (2007). School-university partnerships: What do we know and why do they matter? *Art Education Policy Review, 109,* 13-24.

Carriuolo, N., Boylan, H., Simpson, M., Bader, C., & Calderwood, B. (2007). Special feature: Advice for novice researchers who wish to publish their results. *Journal of Developmental Education, 31,* 28-31.

Clark, T. (1994). 100 tips from bestselling writers. *Writer's Digest, 74*(8), 24-30.

Fine, G. A. (1988). The ten commandments of writing. *American Sociologist, 19,* 152-157.

Hamilton, K. S. (1996). *Acceptance of new and junior faculty into four-year institutions of higher education: An annotated bibliography.* Annotated bibliography. (ERIC Document Reproduction Service No ED396619)

Henson, K. T. (1987). Writing for professional publication. *Phi Delta Kappa Fastback #262.* Bloomington, IN: Phi Delta Kappan, International. (ERIC Document Reproduction Service No. ED292110)

Henson, K. T. (1990). Writing for education journals. *Phi Delta Kappan, 71,* 800-803.

Henson, K. T. (2005a). Writing for publication: A controlled art. *Phi Delta Kappan, 86,* 777-781.

Henson, K. T. (2005b). *Writing for publication: Steps to academic success.* Boston: Allyn & Bacon.

Kamler, B. (2008). Rethinking doctoral publication practices: Writing from and beyond the thesis. *Studies in Higher Education, 33,* 283-294.

Lewallen, L. P., Crane, P. B., Letvak, S., Jones, E., & Hu, J. (2003). An innovative strategy to enhance new faculty success. *Nursing Perspectives, 24,* 257-260.

Mayrath, M. C. (2008). Attributions of productive authors in educational psychology journals. *Educational Psychology Review, 20,* 41-56

Morine-Dershimer, G. (1991). Learning to think like a teacher. *Teaching & Teacher Education, 7,* 159-168.

Natriello, G. (1996). Lessons for young scholars seeking to publish. *Teachers College Record, 97,* 509-517.

Neumann, A. (2006) Professing passion: Emotion in the scholarship of professors at research universities. *American Educational Research Journal, 43,* 381-422.

Nihalani, P. (2008). Publishing in educational journals: Comments from editors. *Educational Psychology Review, 20,* 29-39.

Padgett, D. L., & Begun, A. L. (1996). The writer's guild: A model of support for social work faculty. *Journal of Social Work Education, 32,* 237-244.

Paul, J. L., Duchnowski, A. J., & Danforth, S. (1993). Changing the way we do our business: One department's story of collaboration with public schools. *Teacher Education and Special Education, 16,* 95-109.

Paul, J. L., Marfo, K., & Anderson, J. A. (1996). Developing an ethos for change in a department of special education: Focus on collaboration and an ethic of care. *Teacher Education and Special Education, 19,* 133-146.

Perlmutter, D. D. (2008, March). Get another life. *Chronicle of Higher Education, 54*(27), C2.

Rau, Z. (2007). Training in brainstorming and developing writing skills. *English Language Journal, 61,* 100-106

Rechtien, J. G., & Dizinno, G. (1997). A note on measuring apprehension about writing. *Psychological Reports, 80, 907-913.*

Renegar, S. L. (1993). W*riting for publication: Are junior faculty prepared?* (ERIC Document Reproduction Service No ED 369374)

Solem, M. N., & Foote, K. E. (2006). Concerns, attitudes, and abilities of early-career geography faculty. *Journal of Geography in Higher Education, 30,* 199-234.

Sorcinelli, M. D. (1994). Effective approaches to new faculty development. *Journal of Counseling and Development, 72,* 474-479.

Sternberg, R. (1997, October). *Cultivating creativity.* Keynote speech at the annual conference of the Council for Learning Disabilities, Arlington, VA.

Treven, S., & Potocan, V. (2005). Training programs for stress management in small businesses. *Education & Training, 47,* 640-652.

Tysick, C., & Babb, N. (2006). Perspectives on...writing support for junior faculty librarians: A case study. *Journal of Academic Librarianship, 32,* 94-100.

Westermann, J. (1994). Lessons I've learned. *Writer's Digest, 74*(8), 30–33.

Chapter

5

BEING SCHOLARLY SUCCESSFUL IN THE ACADEMY

Robert Rueda and
Lilia D. Monzó

What is there that confers the noblest delight?
What is that which swells a man's breast with pride
above that which any other experience can bring to him?
Discovery! To know that you are walking where none
others have walked; that you are beholding what human eye
has not seen before; that you are breathing a virgin atmosphere.
To give birth to an idea, to discover a great thought,
an intellectual nugget, right under the dust of a field
that many a brain-plough had gone over before.
To find a new planet, to invent a new hinge,
to find a way to make the lightning carry your messages.
To be the first—that is the idea.

~ Mark Twain

Gender bias notwithstanding, Twain's comment is important. Research means answering questions that have not been answered. Those who conduct research know the intoxication of "discovery" and, with it, they know the dissemination expectations of the academy in which they participate in professional development activities. Education researchers have a primary responsibility to distribute "scientific" information and other scholarly products, not unlike researchers in the physical and natural sciences. By "scientific" information, we refer to learning constructed via rigorous quantitative and/or qualitative research methods. One of the more difficult challenges for scholars in higher education—students and their instructors alike—is mastery of the communicative conventions that characterize written discourse; that is, writing used in theses, dissertations, and manuscripts submitted for publication in academic journals. Many students in advanced degree programs have significant difficulty in integrating these conventions into the scholarly products they are required to produce as part of their educational training and professional development. Often novice students in advanced degree programs assume that writing proficiency in nonacademic domains which they may have previously mastered is easily generalized and that little or no new attention or effort needs to be paid to mastering writing (Obiakor, Lomotey, & Rueda, 1997).

Academic/scholarly writing is a unique type of discourse. In addition, there are important differences between types of scholarly activity. For example, writing the thesis or dissertation is a quite different endeavor than writing a journal publication. Because of this, not only do students encounter difficulties in their programs of study, but upon entering the profession they find it difficult to convert their scholarly pieces into manuscripts. In many ways, writing according to the conventions within the academy is like learning a second language. Like any discourse system, it has its own form and function. Although most students are proficient in the conversational nuances and informality of everyday oral language, academic writing requires logical, systematic, precise, focused, direct, and abstract skills that often are not well-practiced. In this chapter, we briefly discuss the different forms and functions of academic writing and address key aspects of the academic writing process. This content is intended to assist with writing within the limitations of the dissertation research and converting it to help fulfill publishing requirements within the academy.

FORM OF ACADEMIC DISCOURSE

Like any discourse system, academic writing is rule-governed with its own internally consistent and widely agreed-on conventions. In the discipline of social sciences, the primary source for these conventions is the *Publication Manual of the American Psychological Association* (American Psychological Association, APA, 2010) and most publications in the discipline of education require and follow these conventions. Although the details of these conventions are beyond the scope of this chapter, those who plan to make a career in an academic setting or who will be engaging in scholarly writing should become familiar with this publication as early on as is practical.

Although the basic mechanics of scholarly writing are important, it is not this dimension which scholars tend to find most problematic. The basic issue is that scientific writing differs from literary or informal writing. Specifically, clear communication, rather than effect, should be the overarching characteristic of writing for an academic audience (see Tip 5.1). The APA *Manual* for instance, places particular importance on the orderly presentation of ideas, smoothness of expression, economy of expression, and precision and clarity, versus clutter.

TIP
5.1

Communicate logically and clearly.
Orderly and precise communication is an important characteristic of good writing.

FUNCTION OF ACADEMIC DISCOURSE

Although dissemination is a primary purpose of academic writing, and presentation of research findings is one of the more common functions served by
it, there are other reasons to write. In addition to empirical research reports, for
example, academic writing includes theoretical analyses, reviews of literature,
and other formats which focus not strictly on presentation of empirical data but
instead on reaching a broader/different audience. This requires the scholar to
convert research into terms that others outside of the scholar's area of expertise
can understand. Indeed, some argue that all academic writing should be understandable by lay people (Obiakor et al., 1997). Although specific issues of
format differ slightly in these types of publications, the general principles of
style related to academic writing, such as clarity of expression and precision,
are still critical and ensure that the quality of the research and the interpretation of findings are not compromised.

Traditionally, the primary audience for scholarly dissemination has
been, not surprisingly, other scholars. Tenure and academic careers, after
all, often hinge on the evaluation of one's scholarly products by peers in the
field. Many scholars tend to avoid nonacademic sources because they may be
deemed to be of lesser value and importance than academic outlets. "Popular"
publication outlets, for example, do not often have the same stringent quality
controls such as those found in first-rate refereed journals. Sometimes they
exist for different purposes, such as to promote a particular point of view, to
create controversy, or even to maximize commercial sales. On the other hand,
pressure is increasingly being placed on researchers and scholars to widen the
targets of their dissemination efforts. More and more, scholars are preparing
manuscripts for more than one audience (see Tip 5.2). Academics are being
made increasingly aware of the importance of the public (broadly conceived)
as a critical audience. For example, research funding is often tied to public
perceptions of the value of research to recognizable and important problems.
Likewise, educational policy is often set through voting patterns that reflect
public opinion rather than research outcomes. Thus increased pressure is
being placed on researchers to think about their work in light of important
social problems and public policy issues (Obiakor & Algozzine, 1995). There
also is strong criticism within the field of education regarding the failure of
education research to impact teaching practice. Although this issue is inextri-

cably tied to policy mandates, there also is increased recognition that many educational practitioners are skeptical about the relevance that educational research has on their day-to-day practice. Some scholars are advocating for an increase in research that draws on the knowledge and experience of practitioners, particularly in designing research projects that address questions of relevance in the field (Erickson, 2001). This tension is likely to increase rather than decrease, and is an issue that those entering the field, and those who have just recently entered the field, have to face early in their careers.

TIP
5.2

Write for more than one audience even when your topic is specific.
Try many publication outlets. In other words, do not put all your eggs in one basket. Spread the word to extend the message.

DISSERTATIONS AND PUBLISHED ARTICLES

Although the practice of writing strictly for academic peers is disappearing quickly, the responsibility to address issues from a scholarly perspective is not. Scholarly or intelligent writing is not evaluated based upon the length of the words and sentences or the obscurity of meaning. In reality, the worth of writing is measured by the degree to which the reader can understand what you have written. Dissertations and articles are two forms of academic writing that require similar but different writing approaches. Submitting an article based on the dissertation is often the first writing experience for many professionals after graduate school. To facilitate such an effort, it is helpful to recognize a few similarities and differences between dissertations and published articles. Key differences revolve around purpose and conventions of writing.

Dissertations are written primarily to demonstrate competence in research skills to a committee of peers and to contribute to knowledge as a result of the process. The format and writing style are structured, focused, and highly academic (i.e., directed by tradition and graduate school guidelines). Most professionals prepare one dissertation and seldom use it as a model for subsequent writing. *Articles* are written primarily to extend what is known in an academic discipline. The strict conventions required in dissertations (e.g., chapters with sometimes redundant content and extensive reviews of literature) are not required in articles. Rather, for journal articles expectations regarding selectivity of content, economy of expression, and restraint of discussion are particularly germane (cf. APA, 2010).

Recently, some scholars have begun to question the usefulness of traditional dissertation formats precisely because of the unique nature of its style that seems to serve no other purpose beyond the dissertation. The critique stems from the traditional dissertation's failure to prepare and socialize students to professional academic writing and the limited audience for whom it is prepared. Other academic fields, in particular some of the physical sciences and English departments, already allow for alternative formats (Duke & Beck, 1999). On the other hand, in education the traditional dissertation is still most prevalent. Suggestions for alternative dissertation formats include a series of articles that would more closely match what journals in specific areas may be looking for, in effect minimizing the reformulation of format, content, and sometimes even data that ensues after the traditional dissertation is completed in the process of attempting to publish pieces of it in academic journals (Duke & Beck). Another argument in favor of developing new dissertation formats (including allowing students in a given program to chose from multiple formats) is more in line with decentering dominant paradigms regarding what counts as knowledge and how it is best assessed. This argument stems from feminist perspectives regarding the need to rethink the academy in ways that include diverse ways of knowing.

Selecting a Research Topic

Two questions most often asked in the context of students beginning to think about dissertations and research projects are (a) How does one generate a research topic that will eventually lead to publishable products? and, (b) What are some criteria that should guide the selection of a suitable topic? The following are guidelines that have proven useful at this stage of the research process.

First, the topic should be important. *Importance* is defined in terms of the literature and theory in which it is grounded. That is, important research extends the current knowledge base and tells the academic world something that is not already known. This is why a thorough and critical review of the existing literature is a necessary first step in the process. Pointing out gaps in existing research, methodological errors, or shortcomings provides a strong foundation for demonstrating how a research project (i.e., dissertation or other study) will fit in and add to the existing related literature. In addition, ideally, research should address a theoretical or practical problem. This is especially critical given the increasing demand to show the relevance of one's research to current educational issues.

Developing scholars should keep in mind that the selected topic should be in an area about which they feel passionate. Projects such as dissertations and writing for publication require a major intellectual investment and significant time and energy. This is especially true at the dissertation stage. From our experiences, many doctoral students find that the dissertation process is so trying in terms of social and emotional investment that, once completed, students resist working with it again. On the other hand, this burden is often eased when the area represents a personal and professional interest.

An important consideration for developing scholars is that the selection of research topics determines what one is perceived to be an "expert" on (see Tip 5.3). For this reason our recommendation to developing scholars is to consider the particular community of practice within which they wish to place themselves. Who are the scholars in the field that you find yourself drawn to and what types of questions do they consider? What approaches do they value? This is a first step in identifying a topic and a particular theoretical framework for that topic.

TIP **5.3**	*Select a research topic dear to you.* Energy and interest communicated in a manuscript carry weight in the review process. Value reviews but don't take them too personally.

There are areas in research that can be unpopular. These areas include, but are not limited to, topics that do not fall within the mainstream curricula of the disciplines; topics that primarily deal with African Americans, Asian Americans, Native Americans, and women; and exclusive, noncomparative studies of any of the aforementioned groups. Although on the surface this may be discouraging news to some, we believe there are legitimate justifications for doing "unpopular" research. One reason is that ethnic/racial and gender groups are distinctive and present significant researchable challenges in society. These groups are worthy of study simply because of this fact. Another justification for doing "unpopular" research is that the absence of a comparison group is not necessarily a limitation. Rather, particularly in qualitative research, focused study on a group can provide more intimate details of behaviors or customs, without imposing definitions from outside groups onto the studied group. Throughout history, anthropologists, for example, have purposely studied distinct groups (Obiakor et al., 1997).

An important source for finding research topics and problems on which to write is the literature in one's area of interest. Generally, topics arise from critical and reflective reading in a given area. Critical analysis often leads one to identify gaps in the literature and other shortcomings that would argue for a study to be carried out. If students begin to learn to read critically early on in their coursework, by the time they are ready to engage in independent research, they will have an abundance of important questions to pursue.

Finding One's Voice in the Academy

An important aspect of becoming a scholar in the academy is developing one's voice. From a Bakhtin (1981) perspective, *voice* refers to the particular perspective from which one views the world and involves filling the words of others with one's own intentions and purposes. Words, Bachtin argues, are always half someone else's. That is, we do not learn our words from a dictionary but appropriate them from particular communities of practice.

As academics, we are concerned with disseminating research findings. On the other hand, it is a mistake to think that we do not take positions and make informed arguments in our work. The difference between academic writing and nonacademic writing is in the sources we draw upon to make our arguments. As academics, our work must be grounded in methodologically rigorous findings. On the other hand, our own view and perspectives, our voices, are ever-present in the research process, from the selection of topic and theoretical frameworks guiding our design and interpretation, to the various choices we make in data collection and analysis. Good writing requires a voice. To merely present findings without a clear argument as to how such findings should be interpreted is to fail to adequately utilize your influence as an "expert" in your field.

An obvious approach to developing one's voice is to read extensively in your field. This should be something not only required in doctoral programs but actively sought out by students and new scholars. Writing without significant background knowledge and theoretical grounding is nearly impossible. One cannot write well by laying out articles in front of you and attempting to one by one summarize their contents. The first step in writing an article is to simply write from your own knowledge base, leaving the task of finding additional readings for later, at the revising stage. This is especially important for developing scholars at the dissertation stage. Often, doctoral students want to hone in on their particular topic right away and minimize the amount of time spent in the doctoral program by narrowing all of their coursework and readings to a very specific area. Although we understand the need to define the dissertation topic early given the emotional burden associated with this particular step, we recommend taking the time to read extensively in various areas of interest and particularly to become well grounded in multiple theoretical frameworks. Becoming an "expert" in your area takes time, not only to do the readings but to actually reflect on these to have a greater overall understanding of the field and the theories that drive it.

The Role of Critical Reflection

The use of reflective reading to identify where research is lacking in certain areas is only one purpose of critical analysis. A characteristic that distinguishes academic publications from other types of outlets is quality control. How is this achieved in academic publications? The primary strategy is to rely on peer review of scholarly products. Every journal that uses peer review lists the editor and editorial advisory board, normally comprising recognized scholars in the area. When manuscripts are received, they are sent by the editor to peer reviewers who evaluate the content from an academic perspective. This includes factors such as the appropriateness of the theoretical basis of a study, the relevance of the literature in which the study is grounded, the suitability of the manuscript for the particular publication, and the appropriateness of the methods and analysis (cf. APA, 2010). Typically, with high-quality scholarly journals, the process is "blind" (i.e., the identity of the author is not known to the reviewers and vice versa). Following the reviews, the editor typically makes a decision on whether to publish the manuscript, asks for revisions based on the reviews, suggests a more appropriate outlet, or simply rejects the contribution. Although the review criteria for manuscripts that are not empirical research reports may differ slightly, the element of peer review is still critical. With other publications, there may be no peer review, and the editor will make an independent decision.

The process of critical peer review should not be seen as adversarial. It is—theoretically—a mechanism to obtain an unbiased analysis of one's ideas and work. Many novice writers have difficulty with this aspect of scholarly writing and the process is seen as threatening. This often results in diminished motivation to write or else prevents writing altogether. What is critical to realize is that, in most instances, it is the ideas that are being held up to critical scrutiny not one's personality, intelligence, or worth as a person. It is important not to take criticism negatively, since it is not directed at you as a person. It is a tool that expert writers use to sharpen their ideas, present their arguments in a clearer or more understandable way, or even to gain new insights and develop new and interesting questions. It is critical to realize that the dialectical process is what advances understanding, and therefore it should be welcomed, not shunned (Obiakor et al., 1997). The process should be thought of as an opportunity not only to improve the particular manuscript but, more important, to improve your writing in general and grow as a scholar in your field. Often, reviews will comment on what is missing or unclear in your manuscript, point you toward new theoretical frameworks, and suggest additional readings. If taken seriously as a way to grow as a scholar, these suggestions can often be incorporated in future writing and allow the thoughts of other scholars in your field (perhaps more experienced scholars) to move you toward new perspectives.

Becoming a Better Writer

Learning to write in the academy can be compared, in many ways, to the process that young non-English-speaking students go through in acquiring English skills. Academic writing can be seen as a second language, a special type of literacy that may build on existing proficiency but differs in important ways as well. It is as much a process of socialization into a "community of practice" as learning new skills (Pease-Alvarez & Vasquez, 1994). What, then, is the mechanism through which it occurs?

One answer emanates from the work of theorists who deal with young children's language and literacy. Krashen (1989), for example, emphasized the role of comprehensible input in low-anxiety contexts as a primary element in promoting language and literacy acquisition. Comprehensible input, in this case, means engaging with text that is understandable and meaningful. In academic writing, this notion can be translated to mean that novice writers should spend a great deal of time reading academic materials of the type they would like to produce (i.e., always searching for models to guide subsequent work). When one develops an area of research interest, reading academic materials in that area takes on a more personal, authentic, and meaningful character. With increasing knowledge and expertise in that specific area of interest, including familiarity with specialized vocabulary, key theoreticians and researchers, and "hot topics," reading should become not only more comprehensible but more meaningful as well. This should form an important bridge into proficiency as an academic writer.

Other language theorists have extended Krashen's (1989) framework to include comprehensible *output* as well (Cummins, 1994; Swain, 1986). In the present context, this can be taken to mean that in order to move from being a novice writer to being an expert writer, one needs to practice writing that involves two parts: writing and rewriting. The easiest way to accomplish this goal is to get involved in projects and activities that will lead to products that can be disseminated to academic audiences. These projects should be given to several people for review before the final copy is issued. Peer review is an important step in the writing process as it affords the writer the opportunity to "try out" the piece on a sample audience before final production. Whether or not the audience can comprehend and logically follow the author's ideas is an important aspect of good writing skills and leads to scholarly excellence. Ideally, these projects and activities would build on the area of interest that the student is beginning to develop and would subsequently lead to theses, dissertations, and other dissemination products.

A final factor to consider is the beliefs one holds about writing, oneself as a writer, and the role that writing plays in important life activities (see Tip 5.4). These are often formed when one becomes a member of the community of academic writers. Researchers are increasingly aware that personal beliefs are an important mediator of behavior. Beliefs about the role of writing are especially critical. Drawing on the language-learning metaphor again, it is instructive to examine the role of oral language in children's everyday activities. In acquiring a first language, children do not consciously "learn language" for its own sake; rather, it is a tool embedded in activities they want to accomplish. In a similar fashion, it is important to realize that academic writing is a tool, that is, a means to an end and not an end in itself. Academic writing should not be viewed as something to be mastered for a purpose external to meaningful activities. It should be seen as a tool to inform, ignite interest, stimulate conversation, and assist in problem solving. It is a step on the road to continuous professional development in becoming a scholar.

TIP
5.4

You must hold positive beliefs about writing, yourself as a writer, and the role that writing plays in important life activities.
Writing is hard work. Be as positive as you can throughout the writing process.

Assisting Others in Academic Writing

Recent advances in sociocultural theory provide a useful framework on which to draw for thinking about the process of becoming literate in "academies." Although an extensive treatment of this framework is beyond the scope of this chapter, a brief description of some key elements can help demonstrate the usefulness of this approach.

Sociocultural theory focuses on the social and cultural aspects of learning and cognitive development. *Learning* is seen as a process in which the learner interacts with a "more competent other," in the learner's "zone of proximal development." This is simply the difference between what the learner can achieve independently in contrast to what can be achieved with appropriate assistance (see Tip 5.5). In this model, *teaching* is redefined as providing "assisted performance" to a learner within the learner's "zone." This model has often been described as an apprenticeship model, similar in many ways to the enculturation process that takes place when a junior craftsperson is being socialized into a trade or profession. The general goal of this joint activity is to assist the learner to move from the initial stages of "other-regulation" to self-regulation. Just like a young child engaging in storybook reading with a parent, the novice takes over more and more of the responsibility for the task until eventually she or he can accomplish it independently (Forman, Minick, & Stone, 1993; Tharp & Gallimore, 1988).

TIP **5.5**	***Enjoy joint productive writing activity.*** Assist people and ask for assistance when necessary. Share the pluses and minuses to make the whole experience more productive.

Tharp (1993) outlined seven basic means of assisting performance:

- *Modeling*—offering behavior for imitation. This might be in the form of reading academic materials or modeling the process of creating a manuscript for publication.
- *Feedback*—providing information on a performance as it compares to a standard. This can be informal feedback by colleagues or more formal feedback such as that provided by a journal editor.
- *Contingency management*—using principles of reinforcement and punishment. Often the professional recognition that one receives for important ideas or scholarly products is highly reinforcing, especially in the early stages of one's academic career. The punishment for failing to produce scholarly works often means denial of promotion and/or tenure in the academic setting.
- *Instruction*—ascertaining which specific actions are necessary to complete a task. Sometimes direct instruction in the context of producing a meaningful product is the best means of assisting one's writing. Instruction can refer to the organization of ideas, format (especially when writing for a specific publisher), or other aspects such as suitability of topic for specific audiences.
- *Questioning*—requesting a response from impartial readers/reviewers. Sometimes, the questions one receives in the course of formal or informal feedback are excellent means of improving one's written products.
- *Cognitive structuring*—providing explanations to questions raised by outside readers. This can help the writer organize and justify new learning and belief structures. It also makes the writer actively think about what has been written and how it can be improved.
- *Task structuring*—chunking, segregating, sequencing, or otherwise structuring a task into or from components. After the pertinent questions have been answered and the author has mentally reviewed

the project, this is the final step in the writing process. The organization of the document may need altering in order to present a fluid, coherent final product.

In the context of coaching one to become an experienced or expert writer, the best means of providing the types of assistance outlined previously is within the context of joint productive activity—namely, a piece of academic writing. The type and amount of assisted performance provided will necessarily depend upon close monitoring of the zone of proximal development of the individual writer. In general, however, these means of assisting performance provide a useful specification of tools that can move a novice to an "expert" writer.

Feedback from others is an especially critical aspect of this process. It not only helps hone writing skills and thinking, it provides new perspectives that may not have been considered. Although it is not uncommon to react emotionally to criticism of one's work and ideas, it is necessary to keep in mind that the criticism is about the ideas or presentation, and not the writer as a person. It is helpful to think of constructive criticism as recognition of your work by others who took the time to engage the ideas.

Continuing a Work in Progress

After finishing the dissertation, the scholar may find it to his or her advantage to begin looking at publishing opportunities. The best place to start would be with the dissertation itself. Although this sounds daunting in the beginning, one must consider the more positive aspects of this task (a) The topic has already been selected, (b) it has been thoroughly researched, (c) it is a topic with which the author is extremely familiar, and, (d) it is almost already written. The three main steps to getting an article published involve conceptualizing, preparing drafts, and finding a suitable source. If the scholar is starting with the dissertation, the conceptualizing and some of the writing are already done.

What needs to be accomplished in transforming a dissertation into an article is putting what is already written into a more appropriate form. More often than not, the dissertation has a very narrow focus, a language that is common only among the professionals within the field, and an extensive section dedicated solely to the review of previous literature related to the subject. How can one modify the dissertation in a form for future publication?

- *Amplify the context of your research.* The layperson usually wants to know not so much how the research was conducted, but why. It also helps to personalize the research by using language that more easily tells a story instead of states the facts. Using this method allows for more personal observation and helps the reader relate more readily to the topic.

- *Modify the literature review.* Simply put, if it is not directly associated with what you are trying to say, delete it. An extensive literature review, to anyone, (but especially laypeople), is exhausting and boring. The style of a manuscript must flow to keep the reader interested. Weighing the reader down with what researchers said or did many years ago will motivate the reader to quit reading. The author must present importance, need, and relevance with enough breadth and clarity so the study will be understood by a wide professional audience. Also consider optimizing the focus of the Method section. Although extremely important in academic writing, the details of how the author conducted the research (e.g., who was contacted, the details of letters requesting permission, committee forms) are usually not considered appropriate or essential in a journal article. If there is a question about relevance or need, authors often suggest they be contacted for additional details.

- *Minimize tables, footnotes, and quotations.* In order to achieve a smooth, flowing writing style, the author should try to keep tables and footnotes to a minimum. Placing tables and footnotes in the center of the manuscript, on the page following its reference, or at the bottom of the page distracts the reader and interrupts the reading process. Place the tables in the back if you find that they are absolutely necessary. Instead of footnotes, try endnotes. Quotations should be minimized as they, too, can distract the reader.

After making changes, it is always a good idea to have other people, within and outside of author's field, read the text. These reviewers should provide critical feedback on the manuscript's strongest and weakest points, suggestions for improving the overall readability of the text, errors in punctuation or grammar, and comments about the organization of the manuscript. This feedback will prove beneficial to the author in making necessary changes and with ensuring that the quality of the work is not understated.

The public audience is a growing entity with regard to academic writing. It might serve the author/researcher well in terms of further research funding to tailor the manuscript so that both the public and academic audiences can appreciate it. Learning to write while "straddling the fence" will be difficult at first; however, with the aid of those colleagues who are already published, the developing author/researcher will be able to learn and make the transition more easily. The key is to identify scholars who have been successful in effectively communicating to varying audiences and to model one's work in a similar fashion.

PERSPECTIVE

We believe writers are made, not born. There are many strategies one can use to develop as a writer. Even though one may be proficient in some areas of writing, there are special conventions and purposes for academic writing requiring special attention. When one realizes that writing is an important tool that facilitates participation in the academic community, sees peer review as a way to enhance the clarity and power of one's ideas, and actively pursues important and personally meaningful questions and issues, the challenge of mastering academic writing is much more surmountable. In essence, we believe good writing is a critical element of good scholarship and professional development; we also believe there are more reasons to write than reasons not to write.

Writing for the academy is unlike other forms of expression. With practice and a little help from our friends, it can be a positive, rewarding experience. The goal is simple: Share discovery with clear, precise communication; the outcome is unbound.

REFERENCES

American Psychological Association. (2010). *Publication manual of the American Psychological Association*. (6th ed.). Washington, DC: Author.

Bakhtin, M. M. (1981). *The dialogic imagination: Four essays* (C. Emerson, & M. Holquist, Trans.), Austin, TX: University of Texas Press.

Cummins, J. (1994). Knowledge, power, and identity in teaching English as a second language. In F. Cenesee (Ed.), *Educating second language children: The whole child, the whole curriculum, the whole community* (pp. 33-58). New York: Cambridge University Press.

Duke, N. K., & Beck, S. W. (1999). Education should consider alternative formats for the dissertation. *Educational Researcher, 28,* 31-36.

Erickson, F. (2001, April). *From research "on" teaching to research "in" teaching: How I have been learning to collaborate with teachers in the portrayal of their work*. Paper presented at the annual meeting of the American Educational Research Association, Seattle, WA.

Forman, E. A., Minick, N., & Stone, C. A. (Eds.). (1993). *Contexts for learning: Sociocultural dynamics in children's development*. New York: Oxford University Press.

Krashen, S. (1989). *Language acquisition and language education.* New York: Prentice-Hall.

Obiakor, F. E., & Algozzine, B. (1995). *Managing problem behaviors: Perspectives for general and special educators.* Dubuque, IA: Kendall/Hunt.

Obiakor, F. E., Lomotey, K., & Rueda, R. (1997, January). *Writing for publication.* Paper presented at the Multicultural Symposium of the Division for Culturally and Linguistically Diverse Exceptional Learners, Council for Exceptional Children, New Orleans, LA.

Pease-Alvarez, C., & Vasquez, O. (1994). Language socialization in ethnic minority communities. In F. Genesee (Ed.), *Educating second language children: The whole child, the whole curriculum, the whole community* (pp. 82-102). New York: Cambridge University Press.

Swain, M. (1986). Communicative competence: Some roles of comprehensible input and comprehensible output in its development. In J. Cummins & M. Swain (Eds.), *Bilingualism in education: Aspects of theory, research and practice.* London, Longman.

Tharp, R. (1993). Institutional and social context of educational practice and reform. In E. A. Forman, N. Minick, & C. A. Stone (Eds.), *Contexts for learning: Sociocultural dynamics in children's development* (pp. 269-282). New York: Oxford University Press.

Tharp, R. C., & Gallimore, R. (1988). *Rousing minds to life: Teaching, learning, and schooling in a social context.* New York: Cambridge University Press.

6

WRITING BOOKS, MATERIALS, AND OTHER PROFESSIONAL PRODUCTS

James R. Patton
and Stefani R. Roth

If you've not reached where you're going, you should keep going.

~ Festus Obiakor

"**Y**ou *should keep going.*" Doesn't that sound exciting? Throughout this book you have been reminded that once you begin to publish, you launch yourself onto a path for which you will become recognized. There is nothing sadder than to come to the end of a career and realize that you never quite reached your destination (i.e., all the effort you expended and the reputation you have built is not really in the area of your passion). Often, we follow someone else's path because a dissertation or some other project launched us in that direction. There is nothing more rewarding than being creative in the area of your passion: You will not mind crafting your work to the highest level of clarity and impeccability when you love the work that you are doing. With this caveat, you are ready for some tips on publishing your professional work.

TYPICAL SCENARIO

You may have published a number of research articles in your area of expertise but feel the desire to translate the information you've gathered into a product that administrators, teachers, or parents can use. When effective and easily employable "best practices" are presented in everyday language, they become the most sought-after products—but these types of products may be harder to develop than you think if you have been schooled in the style and language of the researcher. With commitment and determination, however, this barrier can be overcome. The enticing question continues to be: Who is in a better position to tell what works than you?

Let's assume you have been doing research in the area of transition skills and you have isolated five skills that seem to be essential for successful transitioning to adult life. One of those skills has to do with the use of technology for competitive employment. You have done a search for products for teachers in various vocational and computer databases. You have searched other databases for reports from federally funded projects designed to equip students with disabilities with basic computer skills, and you have found limited resources in this area. You are pretty sure that there is a need for a curriculum that will help students with cognitive disabilities master some basic computer skills that will allow them to perform several routine jobs required by most businesses. You have conducted a study with a group of students with severe learning disabilities and mild intellectual disabilities and are convinced that it is possible for these students to learn what they need to be competitive. You have even outlined a curriculum that focuses on the essential skills for data entry. These ideas appear to be very marketable. So, where do you take them for publication? You should submit your idea or product to publishers who market to the special education teacher or administrator, and, more specifically, to publishers already specializing in curricular products that deal with life skills and work skills. The remainder of this chapter provides guidelines for accomplishing the task of getting your ideas from concept to creation.

SUBMITTING YOUR PRODUCT OR IDEA

Finding a Potential Publisher

Once you have an idea about the area of the profession where you want to make your mark, you need to find a publisher that includes your niche in their line of products. As part of your early informal planning process, write down clear statements that identify the *who, what, where, when, how,* and *why* about your product. This informational exercise will help you create a stronger prospectus and, much like drafting a thesis, will help you strengthen your own understanding of your product and lead to creating the best product you can (Tip 6.1):

- *Who* is the target audience? Who would want this information?
- *What* do I want to communicate to the audience? What will the end product (e.g., book, CD, software) look like?
- *Where* would this product be sold? Where would the instruction take place?
- *When* will I be able to complete the manuscript? When will the product be available?
- *How* long will this information be relevant? How will I meet the publisher's deadlines?

- *Why* is there a need for this information? Why are there so few books on the subject?

TIP
6.1

Make sure you thoroughly understand your product and the audience you intend to serve.
Understanding the various attributes of your product will enable you to accurately communicate its value to the publisher.

Ultimately, it is the breadth-of-audience factor that weighs heavily in most publication decisions. If no one will buy the product, no matter the quality, it is unlikely a publisher will pick it up. You also need to determine and analyze other materials comparable to yours. The fact that other materials exist should not necessarily deter you in pursuing your publication dream; however, it is important to distinguish what makes your product different.

Although many publishers in special education or other fields are well known to most professionals, it helps to do a little research (Tip 6.2). In collecting resources in your area of interest, you have already established a personal library of books and articles; the references in these resources can provide the names of companies that publish in your area of interest. A range of different types of publishers exists: In addition to established commercial publishers, small publishing houses as well as associations and college-based publishers are viable outlets for your proposed product. A very important point is that every publisher has specific primary and secondary markets; you can get a good feel for this by checking out publishers' print or online catalogs. Once you've clearly established the audience for your product, you should select a publisher who considers this audience a primary market.

TIP
6.2

Conduct research to identify publishers suitable for the kind of work you intend to publish.
Preferences are an important part of commercial publishing decisions. Don't go about the business of writing without important information.

Initial Contact

Publishers are always eager to find new product ideas that will complement an already successful product line. Even though the probability of an unsolicited manuscript eventually being published is low, you can enhance your chances by using the results of your research of potential publishers. The reason many product ideas are rejected as soon as they arrive at a publisher's office is that they do not match the product lines of a company, or the description of the product is unclear to the reviewer. We recommend that you select several potential publishers and lay out a sample section from your materials that is modeled along the lines of the products they publish. However, you should not assume the publisher will see this modeling and connection to their product line—do not be afraid to state the obvious.

TIP
6.3

Take advantage of your initial contact with a publisher to sense the publisher's interest, establish personal rapport, and gain knowledge about publishing guidelines.
Clearly, first impressions are important. Use them to your advantage and take the time to develop a personal rapport. Although your initial project may be declined, building a relationship with a publisher may open the door to other writing opportunities.

With a clear vision in mind of what you would like your product to look like, call, e-mail, or send a letter to the publisher. You want to contact the person who is in charge of the acquisition of new products (e.g., acquisitions editor) or, as is the case in some smaller associations, the director of publications. This contact (Tip 6.3) provides you the opportunity to (a) determine very quickly whether your product fits the publisher; (b) sense the initial interest of the publisher in your product; (c) establish a personal contact within the publishing company; and (d) obtain guidelines for submitting a prospectus (i.e., document containing information about your proposed product) and other relevant information about the company (e.g., a style sheet, a company mission statement, strategic plan, or list of topics targeted for publication).

If a publisher does not have a style sheet or guidelines for developing a prospectus, you should follow the style set forth in the *Publication Manual of the American Psychological Association, Sixth Edition* (2010). Your prospectus should include the title of the product; overview of material (purpose, rationale, and scope); target audience(s); table of contents (including outlines of proposed chapters or sections, if possible, and list of contributors, if an edited work); significant features of the material; comparison to competing materials; estimated length of finished product; and estimated completion date.

Submitting a Prospectus

Your submission should include a cover letter, the prospectus, samples of the material, and information related to qualifications of the author(s). You need to be meticulous about your submission and be sure that there are no typos in the material you are sending. Professional editors see those kinds of details like no others, and careless errors will bring into question the impeccability of your entire project. The cover letter provides an opportunity to reintroduce your idea (if you have had previous contact) or introduce your idea for the first time (if there was no earlier correspondence). When sending the material to a person to whom you communicated previously, you should be sure to remind him or her of the earlier contact. The letter should briefly summarize the nature of the product you are submitting for consideration and convey your passion for the subject. Additionally, you should indicate how you came to select the potential publisher for your work, elaborating how your product fits with the publisher's existing product line. You might also note how the product fits the publisher's overall mission as you understand it; if you decide to address this, however, be sure you are knowledgeable, basing your comments on a published mission statement or on your knowledge of the publisher's other products.

The packet you submit to publishers must respond to the following questions:

- *What* is the general topic area(s) of your proposed product?
- *How* does the topic fit the publisher's product line?
- *What* do you want the publishers to learn?
- *Why* do you think there is a need for the product?
- *What* products are already available on this topic? How is yours different? What is the source of the content?
- *What* is your personal experience/expertise in this area?
- *How* will people use the product, (e.g., curriculum, reference, training manual)?
- *Why* would the selected publisher be the best one to produce your product?

In fact, many publishers use forms developed specifically to help them rate a product. These forms may be used internally or sent out in a double-blind process to an outside reviewer for consideration. A double-blind process, where neither the reviewer nor the author names are revealed, enables a more fair review of the manuscript or prospectus. Figure 6.1 is a sample form used.

Sample Review Forms

Figure 6.1

TITLE					
Potential Audience(s)					
CRITERIA	**RATINGS**				
	Disagree Strongly	Disagree Somewhat	Neutral	Agree Somewhat	Agree Strongly
Please rate* this proposed publication in the categories below.					
A. CONTENT					
The content					
1. Is based on current research.					
2. Reflects practice in the field accurately.					
3. Is objective/factual/balanced.					
4. Includes field reviewed material.					
5. Responds to the needs of the field.					
6. Is appropriate for intended audience(s).					
7. Will enhance professional practice advocated by policy and/or standards.					
B. STYLE					
The material includes:					
1. A format that -will appeal to the intended audience(s).					
2. A logical flow of ideas/ concepts.					
3. Graphics that enhance the text.					
4. An organizational structure that contributes to learner outcomes.					
C. LANGUAGE					
The language is					
1. Grammatically correct.					
2. Clear and understandable.					
3. Sensitive to diverse cultures and underrepresented populations.					

Figure 6.1 (continued)

D. OVERALL QUALITY (Circle appropriate response and add written comments) ❑ Excellent ❑ VeryGood ❑ Good ❑ Fair ❑ Poor
E. What new information would this proposed publication add to the body of knowledge available to our audiences?
F. What are the major strengths of this proposed publication?
G. What are the major weaknesses of this proposed publication?
H. How does this proposed publication support the organization's mission, goals, and objectives as you understand them?
I. Do you recommend that this material be published? ❑ YES, publish as is ❑ YES, publish with revisions ❑ NO, do not publish
J. If yes, what would you consider a marketable price for use in a preservice program? For use in a local school district inservice program?
Name of Reviewer
Position
Mailing Address
Telephone _____ Fax _____ e-mail _____
May we use your comments for promotional purposes? ❑ YES ❑ NO

Major Considerations Affecting a Publisher's Decision to Publish a Book or Material

Essentially, there are four key questions that a publisher asks when considering a product. A favorable decision regarding publication will depend on affirmative answers to each of these questions.

Question 1. Does the proposed product fit one of our primary markets?
Question 2. Does the proposed product have merit (i.e., is it good)?
Question 3. Does the proposed product have marketability?
Question 4. Does the proposed product have any features that interfere with its publication (e.g., high production costs and expensive components)?

What can and does happen is that a publisher will receive a prospectus on a wonderful product (high rating related to Question 2) that does not fit a primary market of the publisher. As a result, the decision to publish the product must be a negative one (Tip 6.4).

It is important to note that a well written, sound, interesting, and appropriately submitted manuscript is not the only consideration when selecting products for publication. The preprint costs of editing, typesetting, design (i.e., page layout, cover, and other graphics), along with the costs of printing 2,000 copies of a 100-page book, can total between $7,000 and $11,000, depending upon the detail involved and the physical quality of the publication. Production costs are divided by the number of copies printed so the unit cost, in this example, would be between $3.50 and $5.50. The industry standard for markup is a factor of 7.5 to 8 times the combined production and printing cost, and covers the review process, marketing, overhead costs, warehousing, customer service, royalties, staff time—and, it is hoped, some profit. The price for this product, then, would be approximately between $26.00 and $40.00. The publisher has to make a judgment about whether the product will sell at the projected price. How many units can be expected to sell the first 12 to 18 months (the recommended limit for estimating a print run)? If we take the previous example and estimate that 1,000 books will sell in the first 18 months, the unit cost would increase to between $7.00 and $11.00, and the retail price might rise to between $50.00 and $80.00. Even though some reference books, reports, and textbooks are priced in this range, most publishers would not be able to stay in business if the majority of their titles were that expensive, as most teachers are unwilling to spend that much money on a book. A publisher has to price books competitively with other products of similar size and content within their own product line as well as remain competitive with the pricing of other publishers.

One more thing: The pricing for curricular materials and other products such as tests usually is higher. This is due to two major factors: (a) They are often multicomponent products that are more costly to produce; and (b) the costs of development are higher. These costs are then passed on to the consumer.

TIP
6.4

Publishers do not publish what they cannot sell.
The decision to publish material is highly dependent on the product's marketability.

The Publication Process

Different publishers have different procedures. In general, however, the overall sequence of steps in the publication process is similar across publishers. Large commercial publishers have a staff of editors, each in charge of a different specialty area or product line. Midsize and smaller commercial publishers have a staff as well, although it is smaller and there may only be one editor in charge of acquisitions and product development. Publication programs within professional associations, such as the Council for Exceptional Children, will have a staff person who is in charge of editorial matters. The publication process can be divided into three distinct phases: decision to publish, manuscript development, and production (see Figure 6.2). Each of these stages has its own goals and activities; knowledge of the process associated with each of these stages is useful for potential authors.

Figure 6.2 Overview of the Publication Process

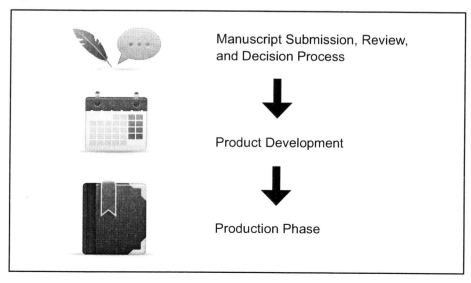

Decision to Publish: The In-House Process

In most publishing houses, the acquisitions editor has the authority to accept or reject a product proposal based on obvious content and marketing factors. Large and small publishers use a peer review process that involves in-house staff and/or outside reviewers. The purpose of this process is to get a reasonable feel for the quality of the proposed product (i.e., Question 2). Outside reviews are extremely important for products on topics with which the in-house editorial staff are less familiar. Typically, multiple reviewers, with expertise in the areas addressed by the manuscript, review the manuscript. Reviewers evaluate the material on the basis of the importance of the topic, clarity, accuracy and validity of the content, value of the contribution to the professional literature, implications for the field, quality of writing, attention to cultural and linguistic equity, and market potential.

If a manuscript or media product has already been developed, the authors will be asked for copies of the material—the number of copies depends on the publisher. The outside review process may take 3 to 6 months. In addition to this field review, publishers generally conduct a financial analysis to estimate costs of development and production as well as the marketability of the potential product. Also determined at this stage is the proposed format and the projected price that will have to be charged, based on development and production costs as previously delineated.

Recommendations of the reviewers are synthesized by the editorial staff and presented to either an editorial review committee or the director of publishing. The committee or director then makes a decision to (a) decline the opportunity to publish, (b) request a revision with a stipulation for further peer review, (c) request a revision subject to approval by the editorial staff, or (d) accept the proposed product. Once a decision is made, the author is notified of the decision and the next steps.

If the proposed material has already been developed, the next phase of the publication process, the development phase, is brief. It quickly goes into a preproduction mode. If the proposal represents an idea for a product that has not yet been developed, the process would take a different route with details negotiated on case-by-case basis.

Product Development

This phase of the publication process literally involves the actual development of an initial draft of a manuscript or prototype of the product. The timeline for development is determined through discussions with the editor and established in the contract. The timeframe for developing a product that is still in the idea stage can vary greatly. Various factors such as marketing campaigns, course adoption deadlines, and conference exhibitions play a factor in setting target dates for the delivery of an initial product.

Generally, a manuscript goes through several stages of revision before it becomes a finished product. Initial reviewers' comments and the staff's editorial judgments shape the product for maximum marketability. Often, title, format, and organizational changes are necessary. The editorial staff works closely with the authors throughout the revision process. Ultimately, an initial manuscript is delivered to the publisher and, in effect, this marks the beginning of the preproduction process. The publisher will usually seek another set of reviews of the manuscript. These reviews are then shared with the author, leading to the development of a final manuscript. The editorial staff prepares the manuscript for production, using a checklist (see Figure 6.3) to assess its completeness.

The Production Process

The production process is typically inaugurated by a "launch" meeting. This is the meeting when the developmental editorial staff hands off the manuscript to the production department. Two major stages are part of the production phase for printed material: preprinting activities and printing/binding. A detailed explanation of the production process is illustrated in Figure 6.3. Some variation will be found from publisher to publisher, but major components of the production process include:

- *Copyediting.* Copyeditor reads the manuscript; queries the author(s) about discrepancies, omissions, and clarifications; and prepares the manuscript for typesetting.

- *Typesetting or layout.* Manuscript is sent to a compositor who prepares the page layout, leading to the generation of page proofs; pages are sent to the author for a final look prior to going to printer— only corrections of errors are allowed at this point; revised pages are returned to the compositor.

- *Printing.* Most production falls in two categories: computer-to-plate (CTP) or digital printing. CTP is run on a standard press, Web or offset, but the files run through an electronic prepress or preflight software and are then transmitted directly to the printing press.

Figure 6.3
Sample Manuscript Checklist

Title	
Author(s)	
Dear Author: We need to know the status of all of the components listed below. Please complete this form and return it with your final manuscript.	
Manuscript	
1. One hard copy	____ Yes ____ No
2. CD/rtf	____ Yes ____ No
Front Matter	
1. Title page	____ Yes ____ No
2. Detailed Table of Contents	____ Yes ____ No
3. List of contributors	____ Yes ____ No
4. Foreword	____ Yes ____ No
5. Preface and Acknowledgments	____ Yes ____ No
6. Dedication End Matter	____ Yes ____ No
End Matter	
1. Appendices	____ Yes ____ No
2. Glossary	____ Yes ____ No
3. References	____ Yes ____ No
4. Author biography	____ Yes ____ No
Permissions	
1. Completed author permission checklist	____ Yes ____ No
2. Signed permissions Release Forms	____ Yes ____ No
Release Forms	
1. Model	____ Yes ____ No
2. Photographer	____ Yes ____ No
3. Artist Artwork	____ Yes ____ No
Artwork	
1. Figures	____ Yes ____ No
2. Illustrations	____ Yes ____ No
3. Photographs Other	____ Yes ____ No
Other	
1. Completed product information form	____ Yes ____ No

Digital printing includes print on demand, where the material is processed similarly to a large-size copy machine. Initial print runs vary from publisher to publisher; however, an initial run of 1,500 to 2,000 is common for a professional book.

CRITICAL ELEMENTS TO CONSIDER IN CHOOSING A PUBLISHER

Different aspects might be considered when selecting a publisher who you would like to put your product into print. Four elements are particularly important and should be considered carefully: contractual arrangements, marketing, editorial support, and production quality of existing products.

Contractual Arrangements

When a publisher has accepted your manuscript or product idea, you will enter into a "right-to-publish" agreement. This contract should describe important aspects of the publishing relationship, including revisions, advertising, out-of-print provisions, termination, death of author, heirs and assignments, waivers, and author costs (e.g., permissions, artwork, and indexing). The contract will also include the date you must deliver the manuscript to the publisher, and describe the copyright arrangement. In most agreements, the author agrees to not publish any competing works for a period of time.

The right-to-publish agreement must include royalty arrangements and royalty payment schedule. In most cases, the author does receive royalties on the sale of the product, typically 5% to 15%, depending on a number of factors. The contract generally also specifies how many free copies of the product the author will receive and any discount that may apply to future purchases. Finally, the agreement describes items related to revising the product and putting it out of print at the end of its useful life. It is important to know that a publishing agreement is negotiable. Publishers use a standard format that can be modified to meet the needs of both the writer and publisher. You must not be afraid to ask for changes to the basic contract if you have good reason.

Marketing

In choosing a publisher, you should consider how your book will be marketed. Publishers who specialize in college texts generally have sales representatives who visit college campuses with samples of publications. They are eager to provide free examination copies to this market. Publishers who provide products for practitioners are more likely to market their products via direct-mail catalogs, Web banners, e-mail offerings, and special mailings.

Publishers appreciate your help in identifying audiences to whom the product can be marketed. Many publishers will request that you complete a marketing or product information form to assist with the generation of catalog copy and other advertisements. Endorsements, testimonials, and reviews that you can secure are useful for promotional purposes. If you provide training or will be in situations where your product could be promoted and sold, you should also share that information with your publisher. However, remember that although mention of your product in a session at a professional conference, as it applies to the topic being discussed, is fine, the hawking or ostentatious promotion of one's commercially available product at such a meeting is inappropriate.

Editorial Support and Expertise

Another key factor to consider in selecting a publisher relates to the editorial staff with whom you will work. Many seasoned authors need very little assistance in the development of their manuscripts. However, most first-time authors find editorial assistance to be extremely valuable. The support dimension implies that members of the editorial staff are available for addressing various questions that arise. It also suggests that various aspects of the development and production process are handled in an efficient and organized fashion.

Editorial expertise refers to the knowledge base that the editorial staff brings to the development process. You want to deal with editors who know the discipline and audiences for whom your product is appropriate. You also want to work with editorial staff that are author-friendly—that is, they convey to you a sense of sincerity, interest, and enthusiasm in what you are doing. Sometimes, it is helpful to submit chapters as you complete them for the publisher to review. Ongoing communication (Tip 6.5) can help eliminate any last-minute rewriting or reorganization of the material.

Quality of Existing Products

The best way to project how your product might look in print is to examine other products the publisher has produced. Although new ideas are always possible due to innovative efforts or a change of personnel (e.g., art director), you can get a feel for production features of products (e.g., organization, format, and cover design) from existing products. This is also valuable for acquiring ideas about how you might want your product to look; some authors identify a type of cover design or a format idea from looking at other products.

Consider the rise of printed material being made available in a digital format. If your book would benefit from making the forms in it available electronically, you should suggest this to the publisher early in the process. This is a time of great changes and evolution for the publishing industry. Many publishers are evolving as dissemination vehicles that deliver to their audience content on many platforms and in various electronic formats. Some publishers are already providing content to electronic readers like the Amazon Kindle™ and the Sony Reader™. Although you may not require a publisher that is on the cutting edge of technology, they should at least have their finger on the pulse and be looking into future ways to support their authors.

TIP
6.5
You must continue to cooperate with the publisher throughout the production process of your work. Be open, but be realistic! Remember, this is a collaborative agreement between professionals. Ongoing communication is essential throughout the publishing process.

SPECIAL EDUCATION TOPICS OF INTEREST TO PUBLISHERS

Companies that publish in the area of special education have distinct topical areas of interest, as represented by the sections of their print or online catalogs. Unless a publisher has determined to discontinue the expansion of a particular product line, a potential author should assume that new publications are possible for any of these promoted areas. You will quickly find out if this is not the case by contacting the publisher prior to submitting a prospectus.

The following topics represent areas that will guide product selection and professional development activities over the next few years, across disability areas:

- Administrative/Legal/Advocacy/Procedural Safeguards/ Funding
- Assistive Technology
- Autism/Asperger's Syndrome/Autism Spectrum Disorder/ Pervasive Developmental Disorder
- Collaboration With Other Service Providers/Co-Teaching
- Cultural and Linguistic Diversity/Disproportionate Representation
- Curriculum/Instruction/General Education Adaptations
- Discipline/Behavior Management
- Dyslexia/Reading Disabilities
- Early Intervention/Early Childhood

- Emotional/Behavioral Disorders
- Family Involvement
- Gifted and Talented/Twice Exceptional
- Inclusive Schools/Classrooms
- Individualized Education Program (IEP)
- Instructionally Relevant Student Assessment
- Intellectual Disabilities, Mild/Moderate/Severe/Profound
- Learning Disabilities
- Positive Behavior Supports
- Professional Standards/Careers
- Reading Instruction/Phonological Processing
- Responsiveness to Intervention/Progress Monitoring
- Standard and State/District Performance Assessment
- Transition/Life Skills/Self-Determination
- Traumatic Brain Injury
- Universal Design for Learning

Clearly, potential authors are not restricted to developing products in these areas; however, these areas have been targeted by various publishers as topics for expansion.

Final Thoughts

We believe the publishing business is rewarding. As an author, you must be cognizant of the following:

- Never feel that your idea is not worthy of consideration. If you have a good idea and you think it should be in print, give it a go.
- Do not think that you must have a Ph.D. to get published. Some of the most practical ideas come from teachers and other practitioners who do not have doctorates.
- Do not engage in "shotgun" submissions (i.e., sending a prospectus out to every publisher in the English-speaking world). It has very limited value.
- Recognize that some publishers have different guidelines for developing a book, material, multimedia, or test prospectus.
- Know that the term *editor* can refer to different types of personnel within a publishing company: acquisition editor, developmental editor, production editor, managing editor, content editor, and copyeditor.

- Follow closely the organizational structure of a publisher's guidelines for developing a prospectus.
- Remember that dissertations rarely make for commercially viable products, unless they are reworked to be attractive to potential consumers in the field.
- Understand that professional publishers are not in the business of looking at your manuscript or looking at your idea for a product, rejecting it, stealing the idea, and then finding someone else to write it. It is a logical fear but one that a potential author has to reconcile; a publisher has to see your material or understand your proposed idea.
- Know that worthy publishers will try to recommend other companies to approach with your idea or manuscript, if at all possible.

REFERENCES

American Psychological Association (2010). *Publication manual of the American Psychological Association* (6th Ed.). Washington, DC: Author.

Israel, D. (1987). *Unbound: A spiritual guide to mastery of the material world.* Reston, VA: Entity Press.

7 BECOMING A SUCCESSFUL GRANT PROPOSAL WRITER

Teresa Mehring and
John O. Schwenn

Getting a grant depends on a written proposal,
and the quality of the proposal and how it is
presented is a critical factor in obtaining a grant.

~ Robert Lefferts

So, you want to obtain support for the important professional work that you are doing? One method is to secure funds from external sources—this means identifying a funding source and writing a proposal. Two external sources of funding are private and governmental; each requires a different strategy. In both cases, you must search for funding sources and represent your ideas in a carefully crafted proposal.

FINDING FUNDING SOURCES

Before writing a proposal to secure external funding, it is necessary to assess your needs and prioritize them (see Tip 7.1). You have to stay focused and clear about what you want, or you will be unable to identify appropriate sources. You must have a solid plan for what you hope to accomplish. Once you have established your need for funding, it is time to search for potential funding sources. This can be a daunting task! A detailed search is a must to determine the best funding source for a particular project. You must understand the funding source and how it works. Private sources are usually foundations or corporations; governmental sources are federal, state, and local agencies. Each offers different opportunities so you must match your needs and priorities to those of the funding source (Bounds, 1997). Each also has different expectations and procedures that must be followed to develop a proposal.

	Know your audience.
Tip	You must assess your needs and prioritize them before writing
7.1	a proposal to secure funding. Match your needs to those of the
	funding agency.

Nearly every foundation, corporation, and governmental agency has a Web page that links to funding possibilities and many give good tips on securing funding from their organization. Miner and Miner (2003) list numerous government agencies and Web site addresses where government grant information can be accessed. More than 20,000 government agency Web sites can be accessed via the main Federal government portal, USA.gov. See the Internet Resources listing at the end of this chapter for some sites that will start you on your way and Web addresses for resources we mention. Note that information from some sources is free, whereas other sites' resources are by subscription.

Federal grants are available from many divisions including the U.S. Department of Education, the National Science Foundation, Health and Human Services, the National Endowment for the Arts, and the National Endowment for Humanities. On a daily basis the *Federal Register* reports details about possible grants and federal activities, including a summary of the project; eligibility; funding amounts; and the name, address, telephone number, and e-mail address of the contact person (Bailey, 2007; Miner & Miner, 2003).

You can subscribe to Web-based notices and documents (e.g., GrantsAlert. com, *Grant Advisor Plus*, InfoEd) and print publications (e.g., *Federal Grants & Contracts Weekly, Federal & Foundation Assistance Monitor, The Foundation Directory*; see also Miner & Miner, 2003) for information on grant opportunities; many of these publishers also provide proposal writing tips that can be extremely helpful. Some subscriptions are expensive, but well worth the cost if a proposal is funded.

Most university research-grant-sponsored program offices have excellent links to funding agencies. University, public, and governmental libraries frequently have resources available in books and pamphlets. Numerous professional organizations have a grant or governmental affairs person who is responsible for securing proposals and giving out monies. Also, as Bounds (1997) pointed out, local businesses and foundations may provide funds for interesting projects.

Others in your area have written proposals that have been funded. Take some time and read these funded grants to pick up writing tips. In addition, attend grant-writing workshops and talk to others who have been successful. Just as using models can be helpful in preparing manuscripts for publication, learning proposal writing skills from successful proposal writers can make the whole process a great deal easier.

Key Proposal Components

Although proposals are always prepared to meet specific grant or agency criteria (see "Proposal Writing Tips.") most include a title page, an abstract, an introduction/statement of need, program design, evaluation, management plan/key personnel, organizational background/history and capacity, and budget (see Tip 7.2). Each is briefly described in this section.

TIP **7.2**	*Focus on the details.* Make sure that in crafting your proposal it includes the important elements of title page, abstract, statement of problem, goals and objectives, methods, evaluation, personnel, and budget. Sponsoring agencies need to know specifically what they will be funding.

Title page. The project title, project director's name, phone numbers, address, the names of the funding agencies, and any required approval signatures (e.g., President's Office, University Research and Grants Office) and assurances are generally included as part of the title page. This page may also include information verifying the project's tax-exempt status. Government grants typically require summary budget information including the amount requested from the funding agency and in-kind contributions from the institution submitting the grant proposal.

Abstract/executive summary. The abstract may be the most important section included within your grant proposal. It should provide a one-half to full-page summary of key components of your entire proposal. It should also paraphrase, in a sentence or two, key literature that supports the need or problem for which you are seeking funding—you should briefly outline what you intend to do to address the need, including methods and procedures, and describe how you will know whether or not your approach was effective and successful. The abstract is probably the first thing (and sometimes the only thing; Bailey, 2007) that a reviewer will read. It should be clear, concise, and specific. You should make sure this section is well-written, informative, and interesting.

Introduction/statement of need. In this section, you should clearly define the focus of your proposal, generally via a brief review of salient literature which indicates that others also believe your focus area represents an important problem. To this end, you should specifically define the problem for your institution or agency. When appropriate, use current statistics (no more than 5-years old unless working with Census data) to document need for the proposal (Miner & Miner, 2003). In narrative form, outline the general plan of action which will be addressed with more specificity in remaining sections of the grant proposal. Back up your statements/assertions with research and facts (Bailey, 2007).

Program design. Miner and Miner (2003) recommend beginning this section with a purpose or mission statement for the intended project. Then include "SMART (specific, measurable, attainable, realistic, and time bound) objectives and a logic model table (Bailey, 2007, p. 70). It's difficult to find a sample logic model table following this link to the Kellogg Web site home page (I have added the reference for the Kellogg publication as well as text citation, here), although a Google search turns up many. We can either assume this effort can safely be left to the reader or provide a sample or worksheet; see pp. 3, 4, 11, 12, 17, and 25 of the Kellogg publication as well as

http://www.thcu.ca/infoandresources/publications/logicmodel.wkbk.v6.1.full.aug27.pdf

http://www.hrsdc.gc.ca/eng/learning/canada_student_loan/images/LogicModel.gif

http://www.tbs-sct.gc.ca/dpr-rmr/2007-2008/inst/fcg/images/logicModel-eng.gif; (see Kellogg Foundation, 2004). A logic model summarizes goals (broad statements that provide the reviewer with a general understanding of what you want to accomplish) and objectives (specific statements delineating what changes will occur) in one graphic chart. In addition to being measurable and performance based, the objectives should generally include short, midterm and long-term statements. "Qualitative, subjective criteria, such as increasing feelings of safety or instilling greater appreciation of art or music may be appropriate for some grant proposals. Like the quantitative criteria, the qualitative need to be well defined. Surveys or interviews are appropriate methods for assessing qualitative topics like music appreciation" (Stinson, Rebouche, & Laughhead, 1997, p. 2). Figure 7.1 provides an example of a goal and related objectives is provided below:

Table 7.1 Example Goal and Related Objectives

> **Goal 1:**
> The accomplishments of the project will be disseminated in order to influence and instruct a wider audience.

- Objective 1.1: Required written summaries will be prepared for the U.S. Office of Education.
- Objective 1.2: Written reports will be provided to the State Board of Education, the Office of the Governor, and the University Research and Grants Office.
- Objective 1.2: A summary of program accomplishments will be presented at the annual state Council for Exceptional Children conference and at the annual International Council for Exceptional Children convention.

This section of your proposal will also provide, in some detail, a description of activities you will conduct to achieve the desired results and stated outcomes. Most proposals restate the goal and each objective in this section, providing a specific description of activities which will result in the accomplishment of each objective, a description of how accomplishment of the activity (and ultimately the objective and goal) will take place, an indication of who will have responsibility for implementing the activity, and a timeline for when the activity will be conducted. (See Fig 7.2 for a sample).

Table 7.2

Program Design Sample
Goal 1—ESU and USD 123 will collaboratively conduct peer coaching.

Objectives	Activities	Evidence of Accomplishment	Person(s) Responsible	Timeline
1.1 Design peer coaching	Grant proposal development (3 sessions)	Written grant proposal	Project Director	8/10- 10/10
	Appoint staff to Planning Team	Planning Team members	Project Director	10/10- 11/11
	Collaborative planning of staff coaching program	Written outline of peer training sessions program	Planning Team	11/11- 6/12

Evaluation. "Grant organizations want to ensure that their funds are well spent and get results" (Stinson et al., 1997, p.2). This section should describe the procedures for determining how and when significant, measurable change will occur. Evaluations can either be subjective (qualitative) or objective (quantitative); (Bailey, 2007). *Qualitative* evaluations might include such instruments as surveys, questionnaires, checklists, and interviews. *Quantitative* evaluations often involve evaluators external to the project and the use of standardized measures. Most projects will incorporate both types of evaluations. Miner and Miner (2003) recommended that an evaluation section include procedures that determine (a) the extent to which the program has achieved its stated objectives; (b) the extent to which the accomplishment of objectives can be attributed to the program; (c) whether the program has been conducted in a manner consistent with the plan; (d) the relationship of different program activities to the effectiveness of the program; and (e) how findings will be shared with stakeholders and disseminated to interested parties.

Management plan/key personnel. Often, grant proposals include a section describing the qualifications of the project director and any other key personnel who will be involved in grant-related activities. The personnel section provides a paragraph or two description of salient information for each project team member (complete vita or resumes are generally included in an appendix or attachment to the proposal). Typical information to summarize: the current position of the individual, including institutional affiliation; the role the individual will contribute to the grant-related activities; and any unique fiscal parameters required for his or her participation in grant-related activities (e.g., 2 months of summer salary).

Organizational background/history and capacity. In this section, you want to highlight the capacity of your institution or agency to complete the work you are proposing—why you are unique, other similar activities in which you have had positive involvement, and why you are well positioned to be successful should funding be granted (Miner & Miner, 2003).

> You must be able to convince the *potential investor* that your agency has been around long enough to manage grant funds, that your agency has the experience and longevity to plan, implement, monitor, and evaluate its programs, and that it has the financial management capabilities to develop single audit trail practices (Bailey, 2007, p. 71)

Budget. Many proposals will require you to complete a budget form provided as part of the application package. In addition, the budget narrative details the specific expenditures associated with the grant request. Budget categories usually include (a) personnel salary and wages; (b) personnel benefits; (c) travel; (d) equipment, supplies, and materials; (e) project evaluation; (f) contractual (e.g., consultants, subcontracts, mini-grants); (g) general operating costs (e.g., office space, room rental, materials, special technology or equipment); and (h) indirect costs. Indirect costs are allowed by some funding agencies to compensate the institution for housing the project if such a project has the potential to place undue burden on institutional resources. Some funding sources do not allow indirect costs; others will specify the percentage allowed. Your institution will want you to seek indirect costs if they are allowed.

For each budget category, indicate the amount of funding you are requesting (direct costs) and any contributions the institution or agency for which you work will be contributing (in-kind contributions). The budget you submit with your proposal is a best estimate of actual costs. The dollar amounts listed in each category should be as specific as possible and should be rounded to the nearest dollar amount. Requests in your budget must have a direct relationship with the goals, objectives, activities, and key personnel described in your grant proposal, and must conform to total budget amounts reflected in requests for proposals or other guidelines provided by the funding agency.

PROPOSAL WRITING TIPS

A proposal must be well written or it will not be funded. A *well-written* proposal reflects high standards in writing and organization—in the view of a funding agency reviewer, it is also one that meets the organization's interest and goals as well as published requirements for applying for funds. A proposal that is stylistically coherent, concise, and well-organized will capture the attention of the reviewer. However, one that is outside the organization's purview will be dismissed, and one that omits essential or requested information will be rejected.

Procedures

Have you done your homework? It is to your advantage to know as much as possible about the funding agency, whether it is a governmental or a private foundation. If you've been monitoring grant opportunities and have become familiar with the various organizations interested in the type of work you do, as described previously, you should be able to match your research interests to a funding source.

Government agencies generally follow annual grant cycles; as discussed, you can subscribe to publications and electronic notifications to keep abreast of current opportunities. They also routinely publish announcements of funded projects; you can obtain copies of successful proposals to read as models for your own. The research articles you read in education journals often cite a funding source; this may provide you with additional leads to possible funding agencies and foundations.

Private foundations fund projects throughout the year; for these groups, however, it is even more essential that your work matches their goals and objectives. Again, you can review reports of funded projects, annual reports of the foundation, or foundation publications to ensure a good match for your proposed work.

For government research grants, your handbook for applying for funds under a particular grant program is the Request for Proposal (RFP) published by the government agency. This document often discusses the agency's priorities and goals, as well as describes deadlines and required content of the application. Use the RFP to develop a checklist for submission; your proposal will not be considered if you miss the deadline or omit a required element—often, if you exceed the page limit for a section, excess pages will be discarded before reaching the reviewer. Most RFPs include a rubric or other indication of potential points to be awarded to various components of the proposal; this can provide you with some guidance for prioritizing your writing efforts (see Tip 7.3).

TIP
7.3

Ensure that your proposal meets the funding agency's requirements.
Be convinced that your project is appropriate for the grant program and sponsor. Use the RFP or proposal guidelines to develop a checklist of contents and establish your timeline for completing your submission. Make sure you include all required elements, both in the proposal narrative and supporting documents.

The RFP or private-foundation grant guidelines also can help you establish a timeline for developing your proposal; work backwards from the due date to break down the elements and phases of compiling the proposal. It is usually a good idea to be liberal in estimating time to allocate to proposal writing. You will also need to provide for time to obtain required signatures (e.g., President, Budget Director, Provost), compiling all narrative elements and appendices (e.g., letters of support, project samples, resumes or vitae—

which may need to be reformatted in a consistent style), reproducing copies (if paper copies are required), and transmitting the final product. It is helpful to compile a proposal-writing team with individuals assigned to research, writing, budget development, editing, and proofreading, as well as support staff to compile the work of these team members and ensure that the proposal is meeting timeline milestones and contains all checklist components.

Do you have questions about whether your work fits the objectives of the particular grant program, or about a budget line item? You can communicate with the agency contact person to discuss components of the proposal. Staff members are paid to answer your questions—if these questions are not easily answered by the RFP or grant guidelines (e.g., budget limits, if not included in the grant materials, or statistical support). It doesn't hurt to request a copy of the evaluation form, which can provide you with an additional resource in prioritizing your writing and ensuring your submission will respond to every item the reviewer is seeking.

Before submitting your proposal, ask a colleague to critically review it in its entirety. A "second pair of eyes" might catch an error you've missed, identifying grammatical errors, logical inconsistencies, unjustified budget items, undefined or confusing terms, unsupported arguments, unfounded assumptions, weak documentation, and ways to improve the overall presentation.

Dot your i's and cross your t's—all blanks on federal and state grant application forms must be completed. To avoid confusion and misunderstanding, write n/a (not applicable) where appropriate. If you are seeking funding from several agencies or foundations, check each submission carefully to ensure that all wording pertains only to the specific grant you are seeking.

What should you do if your proposal is not funded? Ask for copies of reviewer's notes and evaluation sheets as well as a copy of the funded proposal. As with all feedback on writing, this will give you an opportunity to identify weaknesses in your own work that you can correct in the future. Start working on your next grant application! Even if the proposal deadline is a year away, you've gained experience in the process that will serve you well for future submissions.

Content

Your proposal must demonstrate the perfect match between your needs and the work and goals of the foundation or government agency. In addition, it should provide strong evidence of research, staff expertise, and well-developed program models. As with other types of writing, proposal writing is a skill and should be approached as another important writing project that demands your time and close attention (see Tip 7.4).

Think of your proposal as an argumentative or persuasive writing project: Your cover letter, introduction, or abstract (depending on the grant guidelines) should stress the most important point you hope to achieve; your own expertise and the proposed project's innovation, timeliness, and significance; and clearly illustrate why the funding source is the most appropriate agency for the project. You need to establish, early on for the reader, the benefits of your work and why the project should be funded at this time. Emphasize your familiarity with the program and funding agency; quote enabling legislation, the foundation's published words or works, and annual reports to demonstrate how your project fits the intent of the granting organization.

The expertise and availability of your proposed project team is also important. The reviewer is seeking, in your written proposal, evidence of your qualifications. Demonstrate knowledge of current related literature; cite recent sources and include them in the reference list. Similarly, in the relevant narrative section, demonstrate the expertise and capability of the proposed project team, and the appropriateness of your group to undertake this project within the time constraints of the grant.

Write clearly and concisely; eliminate unnecessary verbiage, do not use jargon, and spell out all acronyms and abbreviations at first use. Be cognizant of your phrasing as it relates to gender, ethnicity, and education status references. Write so an educated person from another discipline can read and understand your goals, objectives, and plan of action, without necessarily knowing anything about the particular area of the field or issue you hope to address.

Within the constraints of the grant guidelines, make your proposal easy on the eyes: Use bold and clear, consistent styles for section headings and subsections; wide margins to facilitate reviewer comments; a readable font; models, icons, and/or visual symbols; and tables, graphs, and charts to illustrate points and break up long sections of text. Your proposal should:

- Identify only those needs to which your project can respond.
- Anticipate and respond to possible pitfalls and criticisms.
- Clearly delineate your goals and how you will meet them.
- Provide clear, measurable objectives within an achievable timeframe and reasonable budget. (It may help to obtain copies of the grant agency's reporting forms; the wording in your proposal can then indicate an awareness of the types of reporting requirements and milestones for the individual organization.)

Appendices often are not counted against the page total, so you may be able to append supporting materials and use your page-count limitations for each required section more effectively.

TIP
7.4

Consider proposal writing as another skill to master. Write for a broad audience, use clearly understood language, and tout your own expertise and the value of your project— and back up the qualifications of your team and the importance of your proposal with evidence.

PERSPECTIVE

For many of us, writing a proposal to secure external funding is a daunting task. It may remain so until you write a successful proposal that is funded— and then you will be hooked. Writing a proposal is similar to writing a journal article or a chapter for a book. It is not done overnight but takes many days and hours and needs to be completed with a clear perspective.

When we write a proposal, we think of ideas of what we want to accomplish. Sometimes these relate to particular opportunities that come from out of the blue while others are considered and evolve over many months. We read research and collect related articles. If associates have written successful proposals to this funding source, we read their proposals and talk to them. Some people write better with a team approach while others are more creative working independently. It is always nice to have others helping with the work but too large a group can be ineffective; divide tasks according to area of expertise and provide each other feedback. One of us takes the lead and is the editor so the style remains the same throughout and sounds as if it was coming from one voice. We continually edit and rewrite until it is time to secure signatures and put the proposal in the mail.

REFERENCES

Bailey, L. (2007). *Winning strategies for developing proposals and managing grants* (3rd ed.). Washington, DC: Thompson.

Baner, D. (2007). *The "how to" grants manual* (4th ed.). Washington, DC: American Council on Education.

Bounds, B. (1997). Grant writing for fun, profit, and survival. *CEC Today, 4,* 12.

Miner, L. E., & Miner, J. T. (2003). *Proposal planning and writing.* Westport, CT: Greenwood Press.

Stinson, K., Rebouche, R., & Laughhead T. (1997). Grants: Everything principals want to know. *Here's How, 15,* 1-4.

W. K. Kellogg Foundation. (2004). Logic model development guide. Battle Creek, MI: Author. Retrieved August 15, 2009, from http://www.wkkf. org/Pubs/Tools/Evaluation/Pub3669.pdf

INTERNET RESOURCES

Catalog of Federal Domestic Assistance: www.cfda.gov
Federal and Foundation Assistance Monitor: http://www.grantsandfunding. net/fam
Federal Grants and Contracts Weekly (Wiley Publications; often available via university grant office/university library): http://www.business-magazines.com
Federal Register: http/www.gpoaccess.gov/fr
Foundation Directory: http://fconline.foundationcenter.org
Fundraising and Grants Directory: http://www.fundsnetservices.com
Grant Advisor Plus: http://www.grantadvisor.com/links.htm
GrantsAlert.com: http://www.grantsalert.com
Grants.Gov: http://www.grants.gov
Grantsmanship Center: http://www.tgci.com
Great Source Grants & Funding: http://www.greatsource.com/grants/index.html
InfoEd: http://www.infoed.org
Institute of Education Sciences (U.S. Department of Education): http://ies. ed.gov/funding
Institute of Museum and Library Services: http://www.imls.gov
National Aeronautics and Space Administration: http://www.nasa.gov
National Endowment for the Arts: http://arts.endow.gov
National Endowment for Financial Education: http://www.nefe.org
National Endowment for the Humanities: http://www.neh.gov
National Science Foundation: http://www.nsf.gov
The Spencer Foundation: http://www.spencer.org
U.S. Department of Agriculture: http://www.usda.gov/wps/portal/usdahome
U.S. Department of Commerce: http://www.commerce.gov
U.S. Department of Education: http://www.ed.gov
U.S. Department of Health and Human Services: http://www.hhs.gov
U.S. Department of Homeland Security: http://www.dhs.gov/dhspublic
U.S. Department of Justice: http://www.usdoj.gov
U.S. Government Web portal: http://www.USA.gov
U.S. National Archives and Records Administration: http://www.archives.gov
U.S. Small Business Administration: http://www.ssa.gov
W. K. Kellogg Foundation: http://www.wkkf.org

8 Technology as a Toolkit for Writers

Kenneth A. Weaver

Science and technology multiply around us.
To an increasing extent they dictate the languages
in which we speak and think. Either we use those
languages, or we remain mute.

~ *J. G. Ballurd*

Many people grew up during a time when the writer's toolkit consisted simply of pen, pencil, and a writing tablet. Nearby, the writer's personal library involved a dictionary, Strunk and White's *Elements of Style* (1972), and perhaps, a thesaurus. Conducting a literature review meant spending hours in the library going between the card catalog and the stacks. Needless to say, times have changed. Anyone with an adequate checkbook balance can purchase a computer, access the Internet through an internet service provider (ISP), and a variety of other technological tools for writing and publishing. Although most children are reasonably computer literate, adult writers may not be as well prepared to take advantage of technology's tools.

In this chapter, I examine the question, "What does an academic author need to know about technology?" I begin by exploring the use of a core set of tools: a word processor, electronic mail (e-mail), and Web browser, and provide three examples of the electronic writer at work to illustrate how technology supports the work of the academic author. Finally, I offer a few concluding thoughts on the ongoing professional development issues involved in the rise of technology to enhance the writing of an academic author.

CORE TOOLS

The widespread availability of computers and productivity software affords new opportunities for writers to work more effectively and efficiently than in the past. So, given a new computer with a large empty hard drive, what

Chapter 8. Technology as a Toolkit for Writers **105**

should be on it? What types of software products support the work of writers? What are the essential tools of the trade for a writer today?

The marketplace's continuing development and renewal of products and the critic's never-ending search for the "best" products have caused considerable confusion for consumers interested in learning to use technology to be more effective in their work (see Tip 8.1). Unfortunately, in education, there has been little consideration of tools that might be considered "essential" for our profession. Despite the lack of a common vision about the rise of technology to support academic writing, four tools have gained a reputation as essential tools for students and faculty: the computer, the word processor, e-mail, and a Web browser.

TIP
8.1

Tip 8.1: The right tools make any job easier.
You must be knowledgeable about the core tools of technology to explore your writing strengths. Go beyond the word processor; connect yourself to e-mail and the Internet.

Computer

The marketplace offers a variety of desktop and laptop computers with features that allow the machine to be customized to maximize productivity. For writers, a 17" to 21" monitor displays almost a page of text. The computer can enlarge the text if the writer prefers or speak the text that the writer writes. The operating system plus the word processor software will require a certain amount of memory (note that images require more memory than text; if the writing product includes pictures, more memory may be necessary). For storing, most computers have ample hard drives.

I encourage talking with friends and colleagues who own different types (e.g., desktop, laptop) and makes (e.g., Dell, Apple, and Hewlett Packard) of computers to help identify the most appropriate for your use. There are also books (e.g., Gookin, 2006) and Web sites (e.g., ZDNet) to help the writer identify the computer with the necessary features for optimal productivity.

The Word Processor

Within the writing community, there is little question about the value and importance of the word processing software. It is a writer's fundamental tool for generating, organizing, and editing text. Any word processor will do but be aware that different programs have different capabilities that support writing. For example, Microsoft Word has a "track changes" feature which allows the writer to see a colleague's editing suggestions. However, in my opinion, the best word processor is the one you know how to use and have ready access to. A variety of resources are available to assist in the process of selecting a word processor if you do not already have a personal preference (Acklen & Gilen, 2006; Cox, 2007; Murray, Millhollon, & Melton, 2007).

E-mail

Essentially, e-mail involves using a software program that allows a user to type a message on one computer and send it across a network, near or far, to users on other computers. E-mail provides an essential communication link for the academic writer who requests information, shares thoughts and words of encouragement with friends, or writes collaboratively with a colleague in a distant place. In academic environments you are apt to find any one of a number of products (e.g., Microsoft Outlook, Groupwise) that support e-mail. There are also several free "Web mail" programs available (e.g., Gmail, MSN Hotmail, Yahoo! Mail).

Web Browser

The Internet "is a vast global network of computers connected to each other. Allowing an individual user to access and share innumerable information or communication resources" (Rivard, 1997, p. 1). The World Wide Web ("the Web") is "one area of the Internet that includes not only printed matter, hut pictures, graphics, and sound as well" (Rivard, p. 2). A *browser* is a software product that serves as an interface between your computer and the Web. The most popular browsers are Microsoft's Internet Explorer, Firefox, and Safari (for Macintosh users); many people also access the Web through a service provider such as America OnLine or CableOne.

A Web browser is not functional on the Internet unless you have a connection to the Web through either a direct hard-wired connection or access through a cable modem or dial-in modem. University faculty and students as well as K–12 teachers usually have a free account that provides direct access to the Web while on campus or via a modem from home. Others will need to purchase service from an ISP.

Accessing the Web requires protecting one's computer from viruses, spyware, spam, and adware. Protecting one's computer requires investing in software that neutralizes these programs before they damage the computer, such as erasing portions of the hard drive. Software is readily available online and at retailers.

Checking Technology Competencies

Knowing the components of a writer's toolkit and knowing how to use them are two different matters. Training is a critical factor in moving beyond the basics and being able to exploit the power of the tools on your electronic desktop. Tables 8.1, 8 2, and 8.3 provide self-evaluation checklists to assess your skills in using a word processor, e-mail, and a Web browser. You should take a moment and check your skills. How do your skills measure up with each of the three core tools?

If you are a new user, you may want to use these checklists as a guide in developing your skills. If your skills are in the intermediate or expert range, you should think about using what you know to assist your colleagues. Specific knowledge and skills are necessary to develop the proficiency to use core tools in ways that enhance our productivity.

AT WORK: THE WRITER, TOOLS, AND TASKS

The three core tools we have been discussing are essential to the work of the academic writer because they enhance the creation, storage, retrieval, and manipulation of electronic text. Electronic text is very different from printed text. Text that is captured on paper may be reproduced by copying or distributed by faxing. In contrast, electronic text created in a word processor can be printed, copied and pasted into an e-mail message and sent to a colleague; imported into a desktop publishing program to be made into a handout for class; copied and pasted into a presentation program such as PowerPoint; for use in a lecture or workshop; copied and pasted into a new manuscript or keynote, published on a Web site, forwarded to a wiki, blog, or electronic bulletin board for dissemination worldwide; and used over and over again. A working knowledge of a core set of desktop tools enables academic authors to create, manipulate, and distribute information in support of all the common productivity demands they will encounter with greater ease and efficiency than otherwise possible.

To further extend the list of possibilities technology affords the academic writer, we focus on three common tasks: participating in the academic community, locating information, and digital publishing opportunities, and how the writer might use selected technology resources to enhance productivity (see Tip 8.2).

Participating in the Academic Community

Experienced professionals participate in a network within the academic community that informs and inspires their writing. New assistant profes-

Table 8.1		
Word Processing Self-Assessment Skill Checklist		
Name		
Name of Word Processing Program		
Type of Computer (circle one)　　　　PC　　　　Macintosh		
Check your skills prior to course in Pre column and at the end of the course in Post column.		
Pre	Post	Basic Skills
		▪ Demonstrate how to start your word processor and begin entering text into a new file.
		▪ Demonstrate the ability to change fonts, text size, line spacing, justification, and the number of columns.
		▪ Demonstrate the ability to delete a character, word, and paragraph.
		▪ Demonstrate the ability to insert a character, word, and paragraph.
		▪ Demonstrate the ability to move quickly and easily through a document (up/down, -line, -screen, -page, -file).
		▪ Demonstrate how to access HELP within the word processor.
		▪ Demonstrate the ability to load a file from disk.
		▪ Demonstrate the ability to save a file from disk.
		▪ Demonstrate the use of the spell checker.
		▪ Demonstrate the ability to print a document.
Pre	Post	Intermediate Skills
		▪ Demonstrate the ability to use block functions (move, copy, delete).
		▪ Demonstrate the ability to change margin and tab settings.
		▪ Demonstrate ability to insert page numbers, headers, footers, and symbols.
		▪ Demonstrate the ability to use the thesaurus within the word processor.
Pre	Post	Advanced Skills
		▪ Demonstrate the use of search and the search and replace functions.
		▪ Demonstrate the ability to add lines, boxes, or graphics.
		▪ Demonstrate the ability to use the mail merge features.
		▪ Demonstrate the ability to import text from other programs.
		▪ Demonstrate the ability to format text in columns.
		▪ Demonstrate the ability to use foreign language characters.
		▪ Demonstrate the ability to cite references and use footnotes.

Table 8.2

E-mail Self-Assessment Skill Checklist		
Name		
Name of Word Processing Program		
Type of Computer (circle one) PC Macintosh		
Check your skills prior to course in Pre column and at the end of the course in Post column.		
Pre	Post	Awareness
		▪ I qualify for a free e-mail account through school or work.
		▪ I know how to obtain a subscription for an e-mail account.
		▪ I know where/how I could access e-mail at home or work.
		▪ I know my e-mail address.
Pre	Post	Basic Skills
		▪ Demonstrate the ability to point and click.
		▪ I can locate the e-mail icon on the computer hard drive and initiate the program.
		▪ Demonstrate the ability to enter user name and password.
		▪ Demonstrate the ability to check for new mail.
Pre	Post	Intermediate Skills
		▪ Demonstrate the ability to send one message to multiple people.
		▪ Demonstrate the ability to "blind copy" a message.
		▪ Demonstrate the ability to create an entry in the address book.
		▪ Demonstrate the ability to retrieve an entry in the address book.
		▪ Demonstrate the ability to save a message in a directory.
		▪ Demonstrate the ability to send an attachment.
		▪ Demonstrate the ability to open and view an attachment.
Pre	Post	Advanced Skills
		▪ Demonstrate the ability to customize your mail program.
		▪ I feel comfortable teaching others how to use e-mail.
		▪ I can check my e-mail from a remote location.
		▪ I can set my e-mail's SPAM filter.

Table 8.3

		World Wide Web Self-Assessment Skill Checklist

Table 8.3

World Wide Web Self-Assessment Skill Checklist

Name

Name of Word Processing Program

Type of Computer (circle one)   PC   Macintosh

Check your skills prior to course in Pre column and at the end of the course in Post column.

Pre	Post	Awareness
		▪ I have heard of the World Wide Web.
		▪ I know someone who has "surfed the Web."
		▪ I have used a Web browser to "surf the Web."
		▪ I know where/how I could access the Web at home or work.
		▪ I know which Web browser is on my computer.
Pre	**Post**	**Basic Skills**
		▪ Demonstrate the ability to point and click.
		▪ I can locate the Web browser on the computer hard drive and initiate the program.
		▪ I know how to recognize a home page.
		▪ I know how to enter a Web address.
		▪ Demonstrate the ability to use scroll bars.
		▪ I can recognize the visual cues indicating a "link."
		▪ Demonstrate the ability to select and access a link.
		▪ Demonstrate the ability to use the 'Back" button.
Pre	**Post**	**Intermediate Skills**
		▪ Demonstrate the ability to conduct a search on the Web.
		▪ I know how to obtain "copies" of selected information using the options for (a) Save As, (b) Mail Document, and (c) Print.
		▪ Demonstrate the ability to bookmark useful Web sites.
		▪ Demonstrate the ability to set a Web site as the home page..
Pre	**Post**	**Advanced Skills**
		▪ I feel comfortable in teaching others how to navigate the Web.
		▪ Demonstrate the ability to create a home page.
		▪ Demonstrate the ability to create working links.
		▪ Demonstrate the ability to copy selected portions of html code from a page and insert this code into a personal home page or document (i.e., graphic, animation, format, etc.).

sors often find it difficult to become connected with this invisible college. In addition to having a mentor guide your development and help you make contacts:

- Join a professional association. All professional associations maintain a presence on the Web. In addition, other organizations (such as the U.S. Department of Education) provide online lists and links to associations by specialization.
- Subscribe to an e-mailing list, discussion group, e-journal, e-newsletter, Usenet newsgroup, or forum on topics of interest. "Listservs" (CataList and Aera ListServs are good places to start) disseminate messages to subscribers and provide a forum for discussion; to start; many professional associations also host listservs, online chat groups, and live, interactive "webinars" focusing on specific issues.
- Attend professional conferences. Search for conferences by subject, sponsor, city, state, or date.

TIP
8.2

Stay literate.
Your knowledge of technology can help you participate in the academic community, locate information, and enjoy digital publishing opportunities.

Locating Information

Clear writing requires clear thinking and attaining such clarity is dependent upon access to information such as a journal article or conference presentation. With so much information available on the Internet, how do you find the information critical to your writing? Searching engine such as Google or Yahoo is the answer. Searching is interactive and allows users to continually define their interests based on the search results and information located. Once you locate the desired information, it is very easy to save it (or "bookmark" the Web page) so that it becomes a part of an electronic reference resource for subsequent use.

Specialized search engines such as Google Scholar, provides a simple way to broadly search peer-reviewed papers, theses, books, abstracts and articles across many disciplines and sources from academic publishers, professional societies, preprint repositories, universities and other scholarly organizations. Type in your search term (e.g., the topic of your literature review) and you will receive a list of links to source material that you can pursue or, if you receive too many links, you can narrow your search term to refine the list of links.

There are a variety of scholarly research sites (e.g., Infomine, ERIC, Ingenta, Dissertation Abstracts, and the National Center for Educational Statistics, NCES) you can access and search when seeking information regarding educational research and practice; some are subscription-only. In addition, the U.S. Department of Education's Web site includes a portal to online federal library resources, and NCES provides links to state department of education agencies. The Web also offers a host of ready reference sites. Sites such as RefDesk and the Internet Public Library can provide quick facts or other general information to assist you in gathering information for your writing.

Finally, you can easily access a variety of style guides and guidelines on the Internet. The academic writer often puzzles over questions about correct style. Users of Microsoft Word have built-in access to APA and MLA styles for citations and bibliography; plug-ins such as EndNote make the process easier; and online "citation machines" offer MLA and APA fill-in-the-blanks resources for style formatting. In addition, there are several specialized ready-reference tools (e.g., Purdue's Online Writing Lab, OWL, includes APA and MLA style reference guides; *Guide for Citing Electronic Information; Beyond the MLA Handbook*) to find the answers to style questions.

Digital Publishing Opportunities

Today, academic authors have a variety of alternatives to publishing in traditional print journals. Some of the options include publishing on the Internet in listservs, newsletters, journals, wikis, and blogs which appear only in electronic formats. Electronic publishing is becoming more popular for several reasons. Rather than waiting to assemble a number of articles into an issue or volume, editors can electronically publish an article as it passes through the review process. The information becomes accessible much faster than when published in print. The audience is far larger as well. Rather than mailed just to subscribers, the articles are available to a worldwide audience. Often, there is no subscription charge to electronic publications because the publishing costs for electronic text require no paper, ink, or other materials and no mailing expense. With the opportunity to use graphics, pictures, animation, and sounds, electronic publishing has a greater diversity of modalities to foster authors' creativity and readers' understanding than print. Finally, it is possible to customize electronic journals so as to send to subscribers only an issue's table of contents or only an article's abstract so that their electronic mailboxes are not overloaded with documents. If you are interested in electronic publishing:

Identify electronic journals. Some Web sites (e.g., e-journals.org, Online Technology Journals Worldwide, University of Houston) provide searchable directories of online or electronic scholarly journals.

Create your own Web page. This can be a valuable way to archive your work and provide students and others with access to the information. Many presenters use the Web to provide the visuals to accompany their presentation. Creating a Web page has never been easier. Most word processors will now create HTML code to make your documents ready for publishing on the Web. A variety of programs (e.g., Microsoft FrontPage, Adobe's Contribute Macintosh's iWeb, Google Sites) are available to simplify this task.

Personal correspondence and contributions to a listserv, electronic bulletin board, wiki, or blog join electronic newsletter and journal articles as opportunities to exercise and strengthen one's writing skills and make scholarly contributions. However, I caution you that electronic publishing might not meet a discipline's definition of scholarship (e.g., peer review and original contribution). For tenure and promotion purposes, you do not want to have a scholarly portfolio that contains only Internet publications. Consult with a mentor, your department chair, or dean if there are questions about the rigor of an electronic publication. Nevertheless, there are ample opportunities to publish and flourish on the Internet.

Respond to calls for papers. Monitor *The Chronicle of Higher Education* to stay advised of new opportunities. The *Chronicle* contains a complete listing of events and deadlines for conference proposals, grant proposals, and calls for papers appearing in *The Chronicle of Higher Education.*

PERSPECTIVE

A writer's "toolkit" is simply a set of products that, once assembled on the hard drive of a computer, works together to support the writer in the process of writing. Rather than focusing simply on single applications of technology (e.g., word processing, desktop publishing, and statistical analysis), the goal is to create integration among applications on the desktop to exploit the power of electronic text. A word processor, e-mail, and a Web browser should be considered the basic toolkit for all aspiring authors.

In order to take advantage of technological innovations, continuing education is necessary to stay abreast of new developments to identify appropriate tools and facilitate personalized training to enable you to make full use of an integrated system to support your work. All writers need to make a commitment to ongoing professional development in order to exploit the potential technology can offer. I encourage prospective academic authors to seek out advanced strategies for using a technology toolkit to increase effectiveness and efficiency as a writer.

Finally, as in the first edition (see Edyburn & Weaver, 1998), I conclude with an urgent need to move beyond individual visions to common visions. Rather than allowing technology integration to remain a do-it-yourself project for any writer interested in the challenge, universities, associations, and other professional groups need to foster dialogue about the essential nature of technology to enhance the work of the academic author with toolkits that have been validated by the academic community. Ten years later, we still need to continue this dialogue within professional communities that support the important work of writers.

REFERENCES

Acklen, L., & Gilgen, R. (2006). *Using WordPerfect Office X3*. Indianapolis, IN: Que.

Cox, J. (2007). *Microsoft Office Word 2007 step by step*. Redmond, WA: Microsoft Press.

Edyburn, D. L., & Weaver, K. A. (1998). Technology as a toolkit for aspiring writers. In B. Alogozzive, F. E. Obiakor, & J. M. Boston (Eds.), *Publish and flourish: A guide for writing in education* (pp. 41-47). Arlington, VA: Council for Exceptional Children.

Gookin, D. (2006). *Buying a computer for dummies* (2nd ed.) Hoboken, NJ: Wiley.

Murray, K., Millhollon, M., & Melton, B. (2007). *Microsoft Office Word 2007 inside out*. Redmond, WA: Microsoft Press.

Rivard, J. D. (1997) *Quick guide to the Internet for psychology*. Boston: Allyn & Bacon.

Strunk, W., Jr., & White, E. B. (1972). *The elements of style* (2nd ed.). New York: Macmillan.

INTERNET RESOURCES

AERA ListServs: http://www.aera.net

Beyond the MLA Handbook: Documenting Electronic Sources on the Internet: http://english.ttu.edu/Kairos/1.2/inbox/mla_archive.html

CataList (listserv catalog): http://www.lsoft.com/catalist.html

Chronicle of Higher Education: http://chronicle.com

Dissertation Abstracts Online: http://library.dialog.com/bluesheets/html/bl0035.html

Education Associations and Organizations (U.S. Department of Education):
   http://www.ed.gov/about/contacts/gen/othersites/associations.html
e-journals.org: http//www.e-journals.org
Education Resources Information Center (ERIC): http://www.eric.ed.gov
EndNote (bibliography/citations generator): http://www.endnote.com
Gmail (Google Web mail): http://www.mail.google.com
Google Scholar: http://scholar.google.com
Guide for Citing Electronic Information: http://www.wpunj.edu/library/citing.htm
Infomine Scholarly Internet Resource Collections: http://infomine.ucr.edu
IngentaConnect: http://www.ingentaconnect.com
Internet Public Library: http://www.ipl.org
MSN Hotmail: http://www.hotmail.com
National Center for Education Statistics: http://nces.ed.gov
NCES listing of state department of education agencies: http://nces.ed.gov
   CCD/ccseas.asp
Online "citation machines":
   APA/MLA: http://citationmachine.net/index2.php?reqstyleid=2
   MLA: http://www.palomar.edu/dsps/actc/mla
Online Technology Journals Worldwide: http://www.siue.edu/~yliu/
   online_technology_journals.html
Purdue Online Writing Lab (OWL): http://owl.english.purdue.edu/owl
RefDesk: http://www.refdesk.com
University of Houston directory of Web-based scholarly journals:
   http://info.lib.uh.edu/wj/webjour.html
U.S. Department of Education federal government library resources:
   http://www.ed.gov/about/contacts/gen/othersites/fedlibraries.html
Writer's Reference Desk:
   Yahoo! Mail: http://mail.yahoo.com
   ZDNet Reviews: http://review.zdnet.com

Chapter

9 WORKING WITH EDITORS OF RESEARCH JOURNALS

Martha Thurlow, Bob Algozzine,
Dave L. Edyburn, and
Festus E. Obiakor

Remember the waterfront shack with the sign
FRESH FISH SOLD HERE.
Of course it's fresh, we're on the ocean.
Of course it's for sale, we're not giving it away.
Of course it's here, otherwise the sign would be someplace else.
The final sign: FISH.

~ Peggy Noonan

Some editors sure have a way with words. They should be viewed as allies in the publication process. Don't be afraid to ask editors questions, even though the answers may not always be what you want to hear. For example, a frequent question for many editors is: "Will this manuscript be published?" The unwelcome answer: "Maybe."

What makes a publishable manuscript? How can you increase your chances of having a manuscript published? What are reviewers looking for in an acceptable manuscript? Although answers to these questions vary with the audience (e.g., researchers vs. practitioners); content (e.g., report of original research vs. position paper); and publication source (e.g., research journal vs. practice-oriented journal), a few general tips can be helpful in putting research on paper and preparing any manuscript for consideration by editors and/or other reviewers.

EVALUATING YOUR IDEAS ON PAPER

In addition to addressing questions about audience, content, and publication source, you should think about a few general things as you critically review your ideas for an article. Many of them are related to each other, and taken broadly, they provide a framework for solving problems and addressing key questions related to the publication process.

What Is the Central Theme of the Research?

Your first task is to present an organizing idea or theme that provides a logical framework for your research. This central theme should be provided early, clearly illustrated in text, tables, or figures, and should be consistently evident throughout all sections of the manuscript. Other ideas can be presented, but only if they are significantly related to the major theme. The relation of your central theme to other research and associated theory should also be presented consistently throughout the manuscript. If your work is published, it will be part of a line of inquiry in your discipline and you should make this link obvious, explicit, and exemplary.

Is Your Presentation Written With Simplicity, Clarity, Succinctness, and Parsimony?

A common misconception in technical writing is that complex ideas require complex forms of communication. Too often, professional writing becomes bogged down with technical terms, jargon, and specialized language. Rather than "utilizing prolix representations of Anglo-American phraseology," just "use the English language" to convey what you did in your research. You want the reader to focus on your meaning and not to become distracted by your vocabulary, sentence structure, or ability to use an electronic thesaurus.

Have You Established Logical Consistency Across Sections?

Your task in an article is to make a contribution to the literature. To facilitate this, you should link the need and stated purpose of your study to the present state of knowledge and the specific methods you used to address them. The reader needs to clearly understand where you started, where you went, how you got there, and why taking the journey was worth all the effort.

Have You Developed Researchable Questions and Related Testable Hypotheses?

A manuscript typically addresses a relatively narrow portion of a field of study. It typically addresses a specific set of questions and hypotheses that can be tested with empirical data. There is wide variation in the nature of these data (i.e., quantitative and qualitative), but the hallmark of published research is empirical decision making based on assessments that use tests, observations, or interviews addressing specific questions and hypotheses. Be sure these aspects of your work are clearly evident in anything you write.

Have You Provided Operational Definitions for Key Variables?

The mark of a well-crafted research paper is focused definitions for concepts or variables being investigated. These descriptions should determine the boundaries of inquiry in terms that illustrate parameters addressed or how things were measured or reflected in the concrete steps of your research method. Definitions help you to establish the logical consistency of your work relative to theory and prior research. More important, your operational definitions enable others to easily understand and replicate or extend what you have done. Your definitions (and/or the explication of your research procedures) should be so clear that another researcher can take your article and implement your research even if you are unavailable.

Have You Addressed Technical Adequacy Concerns?

Conducting a research study involves moving from words, ideas, and concepts to concrete procedures and operations. Ideas developed in introductory sections, grounded in previous research and theory, operationally defined, and articulated in specific research questions and hypotheses need to be translated into actions that permit meaningful conclusions to be developed. Scientific concepts, such as adequate sample size, control of extraneous variables, reliability and validity of instruments, and selection of appropriate statistical procedures, must be clearly presented for conclusions and generalizations from your research to be trusted.

Did You Exercise Reasonable Controls?

A primary aim in scientific inquiry is to identify sources of influence related to questions under investigation. The outcomes of any research effort are bounded by the conditions under which the study was completed. To the maximum extent possible, you want to identify and control the sources of variation that are evident in the dependent variables that you study. A variety of methodological and statistical controls can be used. Your task is to convince the reader that you selected the best controls for the environment in which you were working.

Have You Addressed Appropriateness of the Research Design?

Your goal is to convince reviewers that you conducted a study that provides the fullest answer possible to your research questions. The best design for a research study should be obvious once the research problem is clearly stated—yet this design may need to be adjusted because of practical limits such as cost, time, equipment needs, and methods. The purpose for and nature of these adaptations must be clearly presented and the case for the adopted design convincingly argued.

WRITING A RESEARCH ARTICLE FOR RESEARCHERS

Having planned and executed a convincing study, your next task is representing the work for dissemination to a broad professional audience. Systematically addressing a few key areas of professional writing practice will facilitate the likelihood that your work will be viewed favorably.

The first thing to consider when finalizing your research is an appropriate title. The title should be a short (10 to 12 words) descriptive phrase that informs readers of the content of the study. Names of independent variables, dependent variables, and descriptive statements about participants are often used in constructing titles. It is not necessary to include every variable or any outcomes in the title. Good titles include several key words that help others "see" the problem that the article addresses.

A second important part of the publication is the abstract; it should briefly summarize the main areas of the research, including the issue addressed, the subjects and method, and the findings. The remaining content of a research article is usually presented in five sections reflecting introductory material, literature linkages and research questions, methods, results, and discussion.

Introduction and Literature Review

The first section of a research article should introduce the topic being studied, put the study into a meaningful context, and present the problem being addressed. It provides a 3- to 5-page overview of the need for systematic study and the context in which it will be viewed (see Tip 9.1).

First, present general history and development of the problem being studied, followed by a section identifying gaps in the literature that establish a place for continuing study. The rationale for conducting the study is derived from extant literature and clearly links what is known to what was learned in the research. This section can be brief or long depending on the nature and content of the literature that forms the basis for the research. It typically ends with a statement of purpose (one paragraph) that presents the exact questions under investigation.

The key in writing the introductory section is providing an analysis of the relevant literature used to support the need, rationale, and purpose of the research that ends with an indication of the research questions being investigated. This section is easy to describe and difficult to write. The objective is to analyze the literature, not simply report a series of index card summaries of articles or other publications. The following provide evidence that this has been accomplished:

- Acknowledgment of major, relevant, seminal work supporting the need for the study.
- Relations between key proponents of related research.
- Acknowledgment of major schools of thought related to topics being studied.
- Reviews of articles related to key aspects of the research.
- Critical analysis (often presented in tables) of articles, including strong points, weak points, technical weaknesses of previous research (e.g., sample size, instrument quality, statistics), alternative explanations for outcomes, and possible improvements that should be evident in future work.
- Linkages between previous work and the current study (e.g., How does what is known contribute to what was done? How will the current study add to what is known?).
- Common problems evident in the literature that are addressed in the current study.
- Tables summarizing the knowledge base in key areas related to the research problem.

It is essential to rely on primary sources (i.e., original articles or books) when preparing it. Secondary sources, like abstracts or reviews in other works, generally do not provide sufficient information for critical analysis that is the hallmark of a good introduction and literature review. Moreover, secondary sources are someone's interpretation of original research, and interpretations may be biased. When reviewing literature, it is helpful to use a consistent form to facilitate subsequent analysis and summary activities. Generally, reviews answer the following questions:

- What was the purpose of the research and how does it relate to the current study?
- Who participated in the research and how do they relate to the current study?
- What was done (procedures, instrumentation, data collection, design, data analysis)?
- What were the outcomes of the research, and what do they offer the current study?
- What conclusions did researcher(s) offer, and how do they contribute to current work?
- What strengths and weaknesses provide direction for the current research?

Think about Introduction and Literature Review (3 to 5 pages) and ask the following:

- Why is your research needed?
- What are two or three key points the reader needs to know before reading about your research?
- Is your tone positive?

TIP
9.1

You must

- Provide a clear indication of a significant and important problem.
- Provide adequate, relevant, and appropriate background for your study in the literature review.
- Establish a logical relation with previous research.
- Clearly state how the research will advance theory and/or practice.
- Clearly state the purpose and research questions derived from the problem.

Method

The purpose of this 3- to 5-page section of a research article is to provide a description of what was done in the study in sufficient detail to enable others to replicate the work. It is generally the easiest section to prepare because it is grounded in what has been done and less open to interpretation and analysis than any other section. Typically, three subsections are used to describe the research method: description of participants, description of procedures, and summary of the design and data analysis (see Tip 9.2).

The description of participants is typically two to three paragraphs in length. It includes a detailed summary of the demographic characteristics (e.g., age, gender, ethnic group, and experience) of the sample included in the study. The sampling procedure typically is described as well. Special characteristics of comparison groups also should be delimited. The purpose here is to provide sufficient information to enable the reader to know who participated in the study and establish confidence that the sample was representative of the population of interest in the research. Qualitative researchers interested in the study of educational processes typically generalize to three areas: To what is, to what may be, and to what could be. Support for each should be addressed in this section of a qualitative paper to also support representativeness and transferability.

Think about Method (3 to 5 pages) and ask the following:

- Have you described who or what was the sample in your study?
- Have you provided general information describing what you did?
- Have you provided information needed to facilitate replication and generalization?

TIP
9.2

You must

- Describe participants in sufficient detail to facilitate generalization/comparability.
- Describe procedures in sufficient detail to facilitate transferability/replication.
- Describe data collection procedures and measures in detail to foster confidence.
- Describe technical adequacy of data collection measures, including those "home-grown."
- Describe data analyses procedures.

The procedures provide a detailed summary of how the research was conducted, and typically include descriptions of instruments, independent variables, interventions, data collection activities, and dependent variables. Qualitative research concerns for comparability should be addressed in this section of the manuscript. Provide technical adequacy information (e.g., reliability, validity, norms, and scale development methods) to facilitate analysis and replication of the research. The purpose here is to provide details necessary for the reader to replicate the study. In this part of the article, more information is generally better than less.

The design and data analysis section is a brief summary of the technical and analytical considerations that guided the work. This might include a description of the experimental design used, the statistical procedures used for data reduction, a schematic illustrating analysis procedure, levels of significance, thematic analysis methods, and other outcome analyses.

Results

The purpose of this section of the article is to present the outcomes of data analyses in a nonevaluative fashion. The presentation should reduce the data to a series of meaningful statements reflecting the results of the study and should be clearly linked to the hypotheses, research questions, and overall purpose of the research (see Tip 9.3). The section can be organized with hypotheses followed by specific results or with dependent variables used as organizing units of the analysis. The goal is to provide a systematic summary of the outcomes related to the implied or stated purpose(s) of the research. Tables and figures can be used to support the presentation of results; however, tables and figures are used to supplement the text. Refer to every table and figure in the text and tell the reader what to look for, but it is not necessary or appropriate to discuss every element of the table or figure in the text.

Think about Results (3 to 5 pages) and ask the following:

- Are results organized to facilitate understanding?
- Are results presented with sufficient detail to foster confidence?
- Have you considered practical significance of outcomes?

TIP
9.3

You must

- Relate outcomes directly to implied or stated purpose of the research.
- Report outcomes using clarity and parsimony.
- Use tables and figures appropriately and judiciously.
- Provide sufficient information when reporting inferential statistics.

Discussion

The final section includes a review of the purpose and objectives, a review of the key points in the literature review that served as the basis for the research and that highlight its contribution to knowledge, a review of the hypotheses, a summary of the method, highlights of key findings, and a discussion of conclusions and practical implications that have been derived from the work (see Tip 9.4). Illustrate relations between current findings and previous research; you might also discuss problems, limitations, and suggestions for future research.

Think about Discussion (3 to 5 pages) and ask the following:

- What are two or three key points that your work adds to the literature in special education?
- What are the practical implications of your work?
- What qualifying factors or limitations are appropriate?

You must

TIP
9.4

- Derive important conclusions from outcomes of your research.
- Identify and consider alternative, rival hypotheses.
- Link outcomes and conclusions to previous research findings.
- Provide sufficient evidence to support conclusions.
- Clearly describe implications for the improvement of practice.

WRITING ABOUT QUALITATIVE RESEARCH

You may wonder whether guidelines for professional writing are the same if you are a qualitative researcher. Since the mid to late 1970s, qualitative and naturalistic methodologies have gained acceptance, particularly in the social and behavioral sciences. Many authors have summarized the distinctions between qualitative and quantitative approaches (e.g., emerging foci vs. hypothesis testing, process vs. outcomes focus, and rich descriptions vs. statistical analyses). We believe the two methodologies represent points on a continuum, and that guidelines for good writing apply equally to both.

Still, writers and journal editors alike have struggled with how to present and review qualitative research (see Brantlinger, Jimenez, Klingner, Pugach, & Richardson, 2005; Patton, 1990). Reviewers have asked for criteria for judging the adequacy of qualitative research. As you might guess, we believe the adequacy of qualitative research should be judged against the same basic criteria as that used to judge quantitative research. In brief, this involves consideration of the following broad questions and concerns:

- Are research questions clear and answerable?
- Are variables under investigation defined clearly enough to guide data collection and is technical adequacy addressed (e.g., reliability of transcribers and coders)?

- Does methodology match the questions under investigation; in other words, are appropriate procedures used and are they likely to answer the questions being asked?
- Are participants clearly described? Are representativeness and generalizability evident?
- Are data adequate to answer research questions?
- Are procedures for analysis of data appropriate and useful in summarizing findings?
- Are results clearly presented with parsimony and are limitations of the research recognized?

Table 9.1 compares these areas and provides a basis for a set of criteria to use in preparing and/or evaluating a manuscript submitted for publication. Widely accepted standards or guidelines for evaluating the appropriateness of qualitative (or quantitative) research do not exist (Henson, 2005a, 2005b; Huck, 2007; Vierra & Pollock, 1992). Goetz and LeCompte (1984) suggest that addressing criteria such as appropriateness, clarity, comprehensiveness, credibility, and significance of key areas of concern forms the basis for a reasonable approach to evaluating the quality of research (qualitative or quantitative). Table 9.2 provides a checklist for evaluating research reports using these criteria.

Although addressing these broad areas of concern is relatively straightforward, there are other challenges that face authors of qualitative research studies. Perhaps the greatest that we see as editors is authors struggling with the length of their manuscripts. By design, qualitative studies are often grounded in extensive, in-depth data. This is often a strength of this type of research; however, it does not mean that the report has to be long. Goals of conciseness and clarity remain the same in qualitative and quantitative research. Further, the article should be reader-friendly; sometimes this entails constructing a table of broad findings derived from archives, observations, or interviews, or another form of summary. Answering the following question may be helpful in preparing a qualitative (or quantitative) report:

> Have I/we represented the work that was done fairly and accurately in a form that permits the reader to profit from my/our skills as a qualitative (or quantitative) researcher?

Asking a colleague to read your manuscript before submitting it to a journal is always a good idea, and may go a long way in providing an answer to this important question.

	Qualitative	Quantitative
Table 9.1 *Comparison of Criteria for Manuscript Submitted for Qualitative and Quantitative Study*		
Research Questions	General, open-ended inquiries reflecting interest in describing situations and or patterns within them.	Specific, close-ended inquiries reflecting interest in describing variables and/or relations between or among them.
Variables	Definitions of variables are derived from intensive data collection activities.	Operational definitions of variables are derived from literature and linked to data collection activities.
Participants	Targeted individuals or groups or those that emerge during a study that are considered representative of locus or research questions.	Random, purposeful or convenience samples considered representative of population of interest.
Data Collection	Archives, observations, interviews addressing focus derived from broad, open-ended research questions.	Tests, observations, and interviews assessing key components of operational variables.
Analysis	Logical reduction of information obtained from systematic data collection activities (e.g., deriving topics from raw data, developing categories from topics, and determining patterns from categories as indications of underlying themes).	Statistical reduction of scores obtained from systematic data collection activities (e.g., obtaining means, standard deviations, and other measures as indications of patterns of performance).
Results	Narrative, expository-style summaries illustrating outcomes and pointing to conclusions to be derived from analysis.	Narrative-descriptive style summaries and statistical tables illustrating outcomes and pointing to conclusions to be derived from analysis.

PERSPECTIVE

Prospective authors frequently ask questions on writing about research that really are questions about writing in general: How do you get started? How do you know when a manuscript is ready for submission? What do you do when a manuscript is rejected? In responding to these kinds of questions, we usually repeat four basic guidelines: (a) Follow the rules, (b) use a model, (c) get input from others, and (d) do it all again.

Table 9.2						
Checklist for Evaluating Research Reports						
Area of Concern	Criteria	Rating				
		Low				High
Research Questions	Appropriateness	1	2	3	4	5
	Clarity	1	2	3	4	5
	Comprehensiveness	1	2	3	4	5
	Credibility	1	2	3	4	5
	Significance	1	2	3	4	5
Variables	Appropriateness	1	2	3	4	5
	Clarity	1	2	3	4	5
	Comprehensiveness	1	2	3	4	5
	Credibility	1	2	3	4	5
	Significance	1	2	3	4	5
Participants	Appropriateness	1	2	3	4	5
	Clarity	1	2	3	4	5
	Comprehensiveness	1	2	3	4	5
	Credibility	1	2	3	4	5
	Significance	1	2	3	4	5
Data Collection	Appropriateness	1	2	3	4	5
	Clarity	1	2	3	4	5
	Comprehensiveness	1	2	3	4	5
	Credibility	1	2	3	4	5
	Significance	1	2	3	4	5
Analysis	Appropriateness	1	2	3	4	5
	Clarity	1	2	3	4	5
	Comprehensiveness	1	2	3	4	5
	Credibility	1	2	3	4	5
	Significance	1	2	3	4	5

Follow the Rules

Education journals typically require that manuscripts follow guidelines set by the American Psychological Association (APA). The sixth edition of the APA *Publication Manual* (APA, 2010) is now the one to use for preparing articles for most psychological and educational journals. Get familiar with it (and with the specific style manual for the journal that you have targeted for your manuscript). Know the basics and apply them in your efforts to publish your research.

Further, some journals have their own author guidelines that are to be followed in addition to general APA guidelines. It is wise for prospective authors to know what these additional expectations are and to follow them. Start out making a good impression!

Use a Model

Even when you have a general sense of the format of an article, it is sometimes hard to get going. Here is where a model comes in handy. Find an article on a topic similar to yours, ideally one that has been published in the journal in which you want to publish, then imitate what it does. This does not mean that you follow it exactly, but rather that you follow the sequence of ideas, the level of detail, and so on.

Get Input From Others

Never submit an article that has not been read by more than one person. If an article is by a single author, then at least one other person should read it. If an article is by several authors, it may not be necessary to have an additional person read it as long as all authors have read carefully and made detailed suggestions. It would still be ideal, however, to have an objective opinion or two before submitting a manuscript for a critical review.

Manuscript writing always benefits from revision, and that is the point underlying this third basic guideline. Generally, even the best writers put their manuscripts through several revisions. It is best if at least one of these revisions is based on suggestions and input from an objective reader.

Do It All Again

It is more common than not that manuscripts are rejected. However, nearly every manuscript that has been rejected can be revised and submitted to another journal. This should almost always be done.

Perhaps the adage "three strikes and you're out" should be applied here, although even this may be too limiting. Some excellent articles in special education journals are ones that were rejected one or more times before being accepted for publication. The bottom line is "don't give up."

Professional writing is hard work. Many more manuscripts are rejected than are published. Position papers have a slightly higher rejection rate than articles describing original research. Avoiding a few typical problems identified in manuscripts rejected by field reviewers, associate editors, and editors can go a long way in making the whole process more rewarding. Writers must

- Identify sufficient need in literature review or introduction.
- Provide adequate description of participants to warrant generalization.
- Provide adequate description of technical adequacy of dependent data.
- Present results in sufficient detail to warrant confidence and direct strong conclusions.
- Describe outcomes in detail that warrants dissemination.
- Avoid overgeneralization relative to scope of the study.

REFERENCES

American Psychological Association. (2010). *Publication manual of the American Psychological Association* (6th ed.). Washington, DC: Author.

Brantlinger, E., Jimenez, R., Klingner, J., Pugach, M., & Richardson, V. (2005). Qualitative studies in special education. *Exceptional Children, 71,* 195-207.

Goetz, J., A., & LeCompte, M. (1984). *Ethnography and qualitative design in educational research.* New York: Academic Press.

Henson, K. T. (2005a). Writing for publication: A controlled art. *Phi Delta Kappan, 86,* 777-781.

Henson, K. T. (2005b). *Writing for publication: Steps to academic success.* Boston: Allyn & Bacon.

Huck, S. W. (2007). *Reading statistics and research* (5th ed.). New York: Harper Collins.

Noonan, P. (1980). *What I saw at the revolution.*

Patton, M. Q. (1990). *Qualitative evaluation and research methods* (2nd ed.). Newbury Park, CA: Sage.

Vierra, A., & Pollock, J. (1992). *Reading educational research* (2nd ed.). Scottsdale, AZ: Gorsuch Scarisbrick.

10 WORKING WITH EDITORS OF PRACTICE-ORIENTED JOURNALS

Dave L. Edyburn, Fred Spooner, Bob Algozzine, and Festus E. Obiakor

The world can doubtless never be well known by theory:
practice is absolutely necessary;
but surely it is of great use to a young man,
before he sets out for that country,
full of mazes, windings, and turnings,
to have at least a general map of it,
made by some experienced traveler.

~ Lord Chesterfield

Finding the proper balance between theory, research, and practice is an essential part of any professional career. Teacher educators in particular must ascertain the nature of their scholarly contributions to influence both the professional knowledge base and classroom practice. Whereas scholarly training is designed to prepare teacher educators to write about research, significantly less attention has been focused on the characteristics associated with successfully publishing articles on the improvement of classroom practice.

Editors of practice-oriented journals have similar responsibilities to those of research journals. That is, both types of editors perform similar duties: Assembling editorial boards, issuing calls for manuscripts, processing manuscripts, sending submitted manuscripts out for review, making decisions about the publication potential of manuscripts based on the feedback of the reviewers, corresponding with authors, reviewing revised manuscripts, and making publication decisions. On the other hand, there are some salient differences between practice-oriented journals and research journals. Table 10.1 illustrates key distinctions in the overall focus of manuscripts and the specific sections within them. It should be exceedingly clear that a manuscript prepared for a research journal will not be acceptable to a practice-oriented journal, and vice versa.

Table 10.1

Key Components of Practice- and Research-Oriented Manuscripts

Component	Practice-Oriented	Research-Oriented
Overall Focus	Presentation of procedures, methods, strategies, or programs that can be used in classrooms and other applied settings.	Presentation of methods, outcomes, and discussions of original research.
Background	Practical problem and why it must be addressed.	Prior research and conceptual literature illustrating what is known about a given topical area in order to establish the need for a study.
Format	No standard format; typically, an introduction is followed by appropriate sections describing the "what" and "how" of the procedures. Concludes with a reference section.	An accepted research format: opening section introducing problem followed by method (subjects, setting, procedures, materials, reliability), results, discussion, and references, tables, and figures.
Visual Aids	Considerable emphasis on ancillary materials that aid understanding such as photos, suggested readings, summaries of relevant readings, lists of Web sites, etc. These visual aids are deemed essential for engaging busy professionals.	No particular emphasis on visual presentation beyond tables and figures of data.
Outcomes	Typically focuses on the ease of applying the procedure, caveats about implementation, and any data that may have been anecdotally or formally collected as evidence of effectiveness.	Typical presentation of results of experimental investigation which may include tables and figures further illustrating findings.
Discussion	Appears at the end of manuscript, but is not a formal section. Describes advantages and disadvantages of the procedure. May describe implementation challenges and suggest modifications others interested in replicating the procedure.	Appears in formal section of manuscript. Relates current study to previous literature. Addresses problem areas in the investigation and suggests considerations on future research.

The overall focus of practice-oriented journals is—and should be—on practical application. A journal devoted to practitioners (e.g., teachers, therapists, and other direct-line personnel) will typically focus on translations of research into practice, evidence-based practice, and illustrations of how to implement a teaching procedure. This is in sharp contrast to research journals that focus on the specifics of how a particular experimental manipulation was performed and the outcomes of it. Specific sections of the manuscript further illustrate differences in focus. For example, the introduction or a practice-oriented article uses a case study or what is known about teaching or practical solutions to instructional problems as context for the overall presentation rather than a typical research-oriented review of literature. Similarly, where standard formats are used for presenting methods and results in a report of research, the format of practice-oriented articles is diverse, as authors outline "what and how" of a process and describe how it can be implemented. Finally, articles written for practitioners discuss advantages and disadvantages rather than implications for future research, limitations, or conclusions drawn from a study.

WRITING FOR PRACTICE-ORIENTED JOURNALS

Given that any publication cannot accept everything it receives, the editor serves an important gate-keeping function. As a result, it is important that you know about working with editors to increase the likelihood of having your work published. In this chapter, we share our thoughts on ways that authors and editors can effectively work together. From an editor's perspective we reflect on the question: What do authors need to know? We offer advice in five areas, which in our experience tend to cause first-time authors to stumble: selecting an appropriate journal for a manuscript, following the author guidelines, establishing the right focus for the audience, understanding the review process, and responding to revision requests and rejection.

Selecting an Appropriate Journal

Deciding where to submit a manuscript for potential publication is a critical decision and thus warrants some investigative work. We suggest that you review an entire volume year of the journal and carefully look at the topics and format of articles. Locate and compare the statement of purpose or editorial policy (see Table 10.2) for several journals to determine the stated focus of each and the types of manuscripts they solicit. Also, search for the author guidelines and an editorial calendar describing deadlines for special upcoming theme issues (see Tip 10.1). A thorough review of these documents will provide the necessary information to determine whether a journal is an appropriate outlet for publishing your work. When you have your list of targeted journal narrowed down, ask your colleagues, locally and nationally, about their experiences with each journal and what advice they might offer about which journal might be the best to pursue first.

Table 10.2
Examples of Editorial Purpose and Policy Statements

The purpose of *TEACHING Exceptional Children* and *TEACHING Exceptional Children Plus* is to advance the professional development of personnel in the field and to provide practical information, resources, and tools for improving education and services for children and youth with disabilities or who are gifted. Consistent with our purpose, we seek to publish articles that deal with practical methods and materials for use in a wide variety of educational settings. It is an outlet that deliberates critical issues, shares new research and innovative practices, debates, controversial subjects, and advances the growth and quality of programs.

Exceptional Children, an official journal of the Council for Exceptional Children, publishes original research and analyses the focus on the education and development of exceptional infants, toddlers, children, your, and adults. This includes descriptions of research, research reviews, methodological reviews of the literature, data-based position papers, and policy analyses. *Exceptional Children* publishes quantitative, qualitative, and single-subject design studies Articles published in *Exceptional Children* must have implications for research, practice, or policy in special or gifted education. Although *Exceptional Children* publishes research studies that examine the effectiveness of specific interventions, it does not publish descriptions of instructional procedures or classroom materials, accounts of personal experiences, letters to the editor, book or test reviews, and single-case studies Non-data-based reports on innovative techniques, programs, or models as well as studies involving a pretest-posttest only design with no comparison condition are also not published in *Exceptional Children*. Investigations involving questionnaires and survey are generally not published unless the sample is representative of the population being studied.

Multicultural Learning and Teaching (MLT) is a peer-reviewed online interdisciplinary international journal that publishes schoarly works that have research and practical implications. It is an outlet for innovative thought- provoking works in education, counseling, psychology, and related fields.

The Reading Teacher (RT) is a peer-reviewed journal that provides research-based teaching ideas to literacy educators worldwide. RT's articles cover topics such as applying research to classroom practice, developing strategies to help struggling learners succeed, and using technology to enhance literacy development.

Intervention in School and Clinic equips teachers and clinicians with hands-on tips, techniques, methods, and ideas for improving assessment, instruction, and management for individuals with learning disabilities or behavior disorders. Articles focus on curricular, instructional, social, behavioral, assessment, and vocational strategies and techniques that have a direct application to the classroom settings.

Preventing School Failure provides a forum in which to examine critically emerging and evidence based best practices that are both data-driven and practical, for children and youths served in traditional and nontraditional education settings. It is an outlet that deliberates critical issues, shares new research and innovative practices, debates controversial subjects, and advances the growth and quality of programs.

Teacher Education and Special Education is the journal of the Teacher Education Division of the Council for Exceptional Children. Its purpose is to publish scholarly work that pertains to teacher preparation for special education. Examples of manuscripts that would be considered appropriate for submission include: data-based applied research, reviews of the literature, position papers intended to stimulate critical discussion, reports of best practices and innovations that are grounded in the research, and data-based reports of basic research with direct, well-specified implications for practice.

Often authors have a specific question about author guidelines or the appropriateness of a manuscript for a special theme issue. In these cases, authors may want to initiate a "presubmission inquiry" with an editor. These inquiries, either by phone, e-mail, or in person at a conference, allow the author to ask a series of questions while exploring a wide range of issues to determine the "goodness of fit" between the type of manuscript she or he will prepare and the types of manuscripts the editor seeks to publish. Be sure to check the latest issue of the journal to obtain up-to-date information about the current editor.

Submitting your manuscript to a journal is the first step in the relationship-building process between authors and editors. The time invested in determining whether a journal is an appropriate outlet for publishing one's work will pay dividends in the form of thoughtful reviews and timely feedback. A mistake at this stage will waste valuable time in getting your work published.

TIP
10.1
Make sure the journal is appropriate for your manuscript. Search for author guidelines and editorial calendars that identify upcoming special theme issues and deadlines.

Following the Author Guidelines

Most educational journals use the style manual of the American Psychological Association (APA, 2010) as the authoritative source of guidelines on preparing manuscripts for publication. Many journals also prepare additional information to assist prospective authors. Obtain a copy of the author guidelines for the journal you plan to submit your manuscript to and familiarize yourself with the requirements. It is often helpful to create a checklist for yourself to be sure that you have included everything expected for a particular journal (see Table 10.3). Experienced authors ensure that their manuscript arrives at the editor's desk/inbox with all the necessary information included (see Tip 10.2). If you do not receive an e-mail confirmation of receipt or letter within 3 weeks of submitting your manuscript, contact the editor to verify that your manuscript was received.

TIP
10.2

Familiarize yourself with author guidelines.
Make sure your work is submitted in the format requested by the journal (e.g., online submission, correct number of print copies mailed, etc.) and that it includes all the required components (e.g., cover letter, manuscript, tables, figures).

Establishing the Right Focus for the Audience

Articles written for special education and related services professionals typically focus on improving some aspect of professional practice. As a result, authors need to consider several factors when preparing a manuscript that will contribute to the in-service education of practitioners and provide essential information for practice improvement: the intended audience and characteristics of their professional life, change strategies that foster practice improvement, data that summarizes the evidence base upon which the intervention is built, and design standards for communicating information effectively (see Tip 10.3).

Audience. A variety of job titles describe the array of practitioners who work with children and youth with disabilities or who are gifted: special education teachers, general education teachers, consultants, school psychologists, diagnosticians, speech therapists, physical therapists, occupational therapists, paraprofessionals, and administrators. More than ever, their work is collaborative. As a result, authors need to provide insight on the collaborative implementation of a practice improvement strategy.

It is difficult to make assumptions about the skill level and interest of an international audience in a given topic. It is safe to assume that not everyone is a novice who knows nothing about the topic. As much as possible, target your manuscript at a specific skill level (novice, beginner, advanced beginner, competent, expert) and provide sidebar assistance (e.g., gray boxes and marginal notations) as access points for readers at other levels (i.e., *Resources For Getting Started; Advanced Readings*).

Teachers and other school personnel are increasingly facing a variety of constraints and pressures resulting from rapid change, stress, and decreasing amounts of discretionary time. Practically, this means they are finding themselves with little time for reading and reflection. Authors and editors need to identify current issues in the field and assemble information in a form that is interesting, clear, and facilitates implementation. Think creatively about visual aids (e.g., photos, suggested readings, Web sites, templates) that you can add

---

Table 10.3
Sample Submission Checklist

Have You

☐ Prepared a cover letter?

☐ Provided assurances that the manuscript is an original work that has not previously been published and that the manuscript is not being considered concurrently in whole or substantial part by another publisher?

☐ Included the name, address, phone number, fax number, and e-mail address of each author and indicated an address for all correspondence?

☐ Included the manuscript title; author(s) names, position title, and affiliation; and running head on the title page?

☐ Included an abstract of not more than 150 words?

☐ Eliminated author identification information from all pages of the manuscript except the title page?

☐ Opened the preferences setting in Word and removed all personally identifying information from the file, before submitting it electronically?

☐ Retained a copy of the manuscript for your files?

☐ Checked a recent issue of the journal to confirm up-to-date information about the editor and submission procedures?

---

to your manuscript that will offer additional access points for busy professionals to engage in your manuscript. Manuscripts that simply recite information commonly available in textbooks are unlikely to make it through the review process successfully.

TIP
10.3

Increased emphasis on evidence-based practice means your manuscript must describe the evidence that supports the intervention you are presenting. Identify the research-base that supports your work and determine the best way to summarize this evidence for busy professionals.

Change strategies. The literature on improving practice and using research provides a wealth of information on effective change strategies. It is important that authors use this knowledge base when framing the problems of practice. The controlled environment in a research study is substantially different from the typical classroom, and the traditional dichotomy of researcher as producer of knowledge and teacher as consumer of research is a frail change strategy. In contrast, action research and other collaborative roles between teacher and researcher offer significant potential (Ball, 1995; Gersten & Brengleman, 1996; Henson, 2005b; Malouf & Schiller, 1995; Richardson, 1994). Knowing this challenges authors to define an instructional improvement framework and methodology that is "exportable" and one that will produce demonstrable results.

Effective professional development involves a commitment to ongoing learning (Joyce & Showers, 1995). Adults are capable of considerable self-directed learning but need tools to guide their explorations (Candy, 1991). Knowing this challenges authors to create a mechanism for readers to act on their interest in the topic by participating in either organized or self-directed learning experiences.

Learners have different needs at various points in their efforts to adopt and implement innovation (Hord, Rutherford, Huling-Austin, & Hall, 1987). Knowing this challenges authors to describe not only the successful outcomes of a project but to share some of the barriers and roadblocks that were encountered.

Evidence-based practice. The field of special education has felt the effects of recent educational reform efforts and the emphasis on evidence-based practice (Cook, Tankersley, Cook, & Landrum, 2008). Most readers are well aware of the emphasis in the No Child Left Behind Act of 2001 that requires school districts to utilize instructional materials that have been demonstrated to be effective through rigorous, scientifically based research. As a result, journal editors have become much more sensitive to the need to have authors clearly represent the evidence base for the intervention that they are presenting. Therefore, be sure your manuscript speaks to this issue.

Design standards. Given the preceding issues, an editor is challenged to respond by developing design standards for communicating information effectively. For practice-oriented journals, this typically translates to writing style, format, and layout (see Tip 10.4). Ogawa and Malen (1991) observed that the literature tends to be noninclusive of the views or voices of diverse sets of authors. Using techniques (i.e., sidebars and quote boxes) to enable multiple voices to be heard is a valuable asset in creating articles for dissemination to practicing professionals. *Diversity* in this context refers to the array of professional roles, race, and ethnicity, as well as viewpoint (e.g., a parent offers her opposition to an inclusion project). Avoid jargon and "academic prose" in favor of a style of writing that engages the reader.

TIP

10.4

Be aware of your audience, outcome, style, format, and layout when you write, especially when you are writing for practice-oriented journals.

Review recent issues and articles to determine key features of the journal.

The hallmark of manuscripts accepted for publication in a practice-oriented journal is a focus on the practical application of knowledge. These manuscripts have a strong central message and communicate valuable supplementary information (e.g., frameworks, guidelines, readings for further study, profiles of the participants, and quotes or viewpoints of individuals with a major stake in the intervention described). Issues of format must be addressed by the author in developing the manuscript and are not simply a minor revision of a manuscript rejected by another journal.

With the information explosion of recent years, readers are increasingly pressed for time. As a result, journals are more and more using principles of visual design of information (Wurman, 1989) in layouts to make it easy for readers to browse and locate information that is informative and immediately useful. Authors must browse these journals for ideas and inspirations about effective visual design formats prior to submission. Typically, this is a collaborative task between the editors and authors when a manuscript revision is prepared (e.g., there is no need to include photos when submitting your manuscript for review).

Understand the manuscript review process to avoid unnecessary stress.

TIP
10.5
Because editorial work is only part of what editors and reviewers do, there are often delays in the review process. Monitor the review timelines but do not worry if things are a bit slow. Do feel free to contact the editorial office during the review process.

Understanding the Manuscript Review Process

When a manuscript arrives at the editor's office via traditional mail or Web-based submission, it is assigned a unique identification number that is used for tracking it throughout the review and publication process. Relevant information about the manuscript and author is entered into a database. Then the editor screens the manuscript. The purpose of this initial screening is to determine if it is appropriate to consider for peer review. Some of the reasons a manuscript may not be accepted for review include: (a) the focus of the manuscript is outside the focus of the journal; (b) failure to follow the manuscript guidelines concerning length, format, and style; or (c) the specific topic of the manuscript is one on which the journal has already published within the past 2 years or the journal already has manuscripts slated for publication on this topic. Manuscripts are rejected during the screening process if they are so poorly written that they have little chance of passing the judgment of the reviewers.

If the editor determines the manuscript will be accepted for review, an acknowledgment letter is sent to the author with the manuscript tracking number and information about the expected timelines for the peer review. The editor also selects reviewers who will receive the manuscript without author identification (blind review). Typically, reviewers are asked to prepare a written summary of their remarks and return them in 3 to 6 weeks. Authors are encouraged to contact the editorial offices any time during the review process regarding questions about the status of their manuscript (see Tip 10.5).

Responding to Revision Requests and Rejection

When all the reviews are returned, the editor reads the manuscript and reviewers' comments and makes a decision about the manuscript. The options typically involve one of four possible actions: reject, revise and resubmit, accept pending revisions, or accept. It may be of little consolation, but less than 20% of manuscripts submitted to many journals are accepted (Henson, 2005b). Authors who have had their work rejected may wish to contact the editor to schedule a phone conference to discuss the feedback on their work.

Persistence is a key attribute of successful authors. Interestingly, many manuscripts rejected by one journal are accepted by another after revision and rewriting guided by the initial review.

TIP
10.6

Know the bumps on the way to publication—reviewed manuscripts might be rejected, require a revision and then be resubmitted, or accepted pending revisions.
Respond promptly to all editorial inquiries and deadlines. Your performance in this phase of the publication process will enhance your reputation as an author who is courteous, thoughtful, and reliable.

Only a small percentage of manuscripts are accepted without some level of revision. Therefore, authors must learn to prepare revisions by reflecting on the reviewers' comments and making the changes they agree with, and then consulting with the editor about comments that are unclear or changes that seem inappropriate. At this stage, it is important to maintain communication with the editor, especially if unanticipated circumstances arise which prevent you from meeting a deadline. Typically, the editor will again contact the author concerning the acceptance of the final revisions and clarification of any remaining issues. It is during this phase of the process that authors and editors communicate most frequently.

The final phase of the publishing process involves activities associated with production of the journal. During this time, the author may be contacted by the editor, copyeditor, or production editor concerning lingering stylistic issues, copyright releases, camera-ready figures and artwork, and photos to accompany the article. Again, prompt responses to these inquiries are essential in order to sustain established production timelines (See Tip 10.6).

PERSPECTIVE

Most editors recall all too vividly their painful induction to academic publishing. As a result, many actively pursue strategies to assist new authors in understanding the publication process and navigating it successfully. Readers interested in additional information on the author-editor relationship may wish to consult some of the resources in Table 10.4.

Journal editors enjoy meeting new authors. We like listening to ideas about work in progress. We are happy to share our perspectives on how a manuscript might be prepared to meet the approval of the reviewers. We are thrilled when a manuscript shows up in our mailbox. We enjoy working with writers on revisions and getting a manuscript in shape for acceptance. We share the writer's excitement as each new issue is published. In the end, it is important to know: We do not like writing rejection letters.

REFERENCES

American Psychological Association. (2010). *Publication manual of the American Psychological Association* (6th ed). Washington, DC: Author.

Ball, D. L. (1995). Blurring the boundaries of research and practice. *Remedial and Special Education, 16,* 354-363.

Candy, P. C. (1991). *Self-direction for lifelong learning: A comprehensive guide to theory and practice.* San Francisco: Jossey-Bass.

Cook, B. G., Tankersley, M., Cook, L., & Landrum, T. J. (2008). Evidence-based practices in special education: Some practical considerations. *Intervention in School and Clinic, 44*(2), 69-75.

Gersten, R., & Brengleman, S. U. (1996). The quest to translate research into classroom practice: The emerging knowledge base. *Remedial and Special Education, 17(2),* 67-74.

Henson (2005 b) *Writing for publication: Road to academic achievement.* Boston: Allyn & Bacon.

Hord, S. M., Rutherford, W. L., Huling-Austin, L., & Hall, C. E. (1987). *Taking charge of change.* Alexandria, VA: ASCD.

Joyce, B., & Showers, B. (1995). *Student achievement through staff development* (2nd ed). New York: Longman.

Malouf, D. B., & Schiller, E. P. (1995). Practice and research in special education. *Exceptional Children, 61,* 414-424.

Ogawa, R. T., & Malen, B. (1991). Towards rigor in reviews of multivocal literatures: Applying the exploratory case study method. *Review of Educational Research, 61,* 265-286.

Richardson, V. (1994). Conducting research on practice. *Educational Researcher, 23(5),* 5-10.

Wurman, R. S. (1989). *Information anxiety.* New York: Doubleday.

ADDITIONAL RESOURCES

Boardman, A. G., Arguelles, M. E., Vaughn, S., Hughes, M. T., & Klingner, J. (2005). Special education teachers' views of research-based practices. *The Journal of Special Education, 39,* 168-180.

Boice, R. (1990). *Professors as writers: A self-help guide to productive writing.* Stillwater, OK: New Forums Press.

Cantor, J. A. (1993). *A guide to academic writing.* Westport, CT: Praeger.

Derricourt, R. (1996). *An author's guide to scholarly publishing.* Princeton, NJ: Princeton University Press.

Fiske, D. W, & Fogg, L. (1990). But the reviewers are making different criticisms of my paper! Diversity and uniqueness in reviewer comments. *American Psychologist, 45,* 591-598.

Garrett, J. E., & McLoughlin, J. A. (1995). A reference for judging the quality of publications in special education and related service journals. *Teacher Education and Special Education, 18,* 133-138.

Henson, K. T. (2005). *Writing for publication: Road to academic advancement.* Boston: Allyn & Bacon.

Kupfersmid, J., & Wonderly, D. M. (1994). *An author's guide to publishing better articles in better journals in the behavioral sciences.* Brandon, CT: Clinical Psychology Publishing.

Niederhauser, D. S., Wetzel, K., & Lindstrom, D. L. (2005). From manuscript to article: Publishing educational technology research. *Journal of Technology and Teacher Education, 13*(4), 656-692.

Peek, R. P., & Newby, C. B. (1996). *Scholarly publishing: The electronic frontier.* Cambridge, MA: MIT Press.

Silia, P. J. (2007). *How to write a lot: A practical guide to productive academic writing.* Washington, DC: APA Press.

Wepner, S. B., & Gambrell, L. B. (2006). *Beating the odds: Getting published in the field of literacy.* Newark, DE: International Reading Association.

Chapter

11

GROWING PROFESSIONALLY, IMPROVING CONTINUOUSLY, AND MAKING A DIFFERENCE

Bob Algozzine, Festus E. Obiakor,
Bob Audette, and Jeffrey P. Bakken

Once in seven years I burn all my sermons;
for it is a shame if I cannot write better sermons now
than I did seven years ago.

~ *John Wesley*

Continuous review and improvement is a part of the writing process and the rallying cry for important practices driving reform efforts in many areas of American life. W. Edward Deming's Total Quality Management (TQM) philosophy, first used in industry, provides a valuable framework for approaching positive methods of monitoring and change in personal and professional practices. TQM is both a way of thinking and a set of guiding principles for action. Implementing the beliefs creates environments in which groups are viewed as learning organizations with a shared sense of purpose driving efforts toward improved productivity. The principles have had value in transforming failing industries and recently have been applied in efforts to improve education. A foundation of "total quality" thinking is consistency and alignment between purposes of an activity and processes for making it happen. Applying this to scholarship as part of professional development involves bringing goals of writing and processes for producing written work together. Focusing on the following seven areas provides a practical approach to professional development in writing:

- Broad goals and missions.
- Immediate purposes specific to a manuscript.
- Criteria for meeting manuscript goals.
- Plans for completing manuscripts.
- Progress assessment.
- Evaluation of completed manuscripts.
- Evaluation of the writing process and progress toward a mission.

DEVELOPING GOALS

Whether writing represents the totality of a person's career as with a newspaper columnist or is merely one element of a more diverse career such as university teaching, it is valuable to reflect and consider the broad purposes of authorship. Some people write to entertain and sometimes there is a direct relationship between their writings and their earnings. Others write to participate in a discourse on ideas of great importance to them and often increments in income are only indirectly or minimally related to their written products. Still others write to further the knowledge of themselves and others and to directly impact other researchers as well as teachers, parents, and students. Regardless of the purpose, it is essential that the author's mission is clear and explicit. Successful writers have clear understandings of what they are trying to accomplish with their written work. Furthermore, they recognize how their written work contributes to their broad goals and mission, and this helps them maintain a focus as professional development progresses.

In the absence of such clarity of purpose and direction, efforts to write are not likely to succeed. It is not unusual for struggling writers to have difficulty articulating the "why" of their writing. This problem occurs frequently when the impetus for "scholarship" is external to the writer, as in the case of college course assignments or the production of an unspecified number of publications in efforts to attack the tenure and promotion process within most university systems. The importance of mission (i.e., finding your voice) has been well-articulated in other chapters of this book. It is clearly a meaningful place to start when planning a professional development career guided by "quality" considerations.

DEVELOPING PURPOSES

In the same manner that authors need to be explicit regarding their broad goals, it is very important that the roles of what they write in the attainment of the mission are also understood. Comprehension of the goals and strategic value of specific manuscripts will enhance the likelihood that the plans for production are adequate and appropriate. There is a direct relationship between the goals of a specific manuscript and the medium in which it will be produced (e.g., technical journal, book), the audience being addressed, the timing of publication, and prewriting work which must be accomplished (e.g., research). Authors will find that a repertoire of different styles is needed depending on the outlet being considered for submission for possible publication. Knowing your audience and publication format is essential to success. Support for making this happen has been provided in several earlier chapters.

Aligning Goals and Purposes

Goals without quality criteria for attainment are relatively useless. For example, if a goal for a manuscript is to introduce a new idea for the consideration of a specific audience, the following criteria might apply:

- Premanuscript knowledge of the audience awareness regarding the idea determines the complexity and comprehensibility of the text.
- Media focus which reaches the preferred audience determines the target or organ for which publication acceptance is sought.
- Media requirements such as length and style must be well understood.
- Desired actions of the audience may require publication prior to a certain date, as is often the case with special or thematic issues of professional journals.

Successful writers identify and monitor their adherence to the criteria for meeting the goals of their manuscripts; suggestions for doing this better were offered in earlier chapters focused on writing in research- and practice-oriented journals.

Planning Manuscripts

A productive plan for completing specific manuscripts includes

- Identifying the manuscript goals and criteria.
- Considering production processes which have been previously effective for the author and avoiding those which have not worked satisfactorily.
- Establishing production steps consistent with the criteria and past successful processes.
- Setting timetables for completion of production steps.
- Allocating time and resources for completion of work.

Putting any plan into action requires sustained, directed decisions, and actions. For most university faculty, this means deciding how to allocate time to competing priorities. It also means spending time writing and revising manuscripts to be submitted for publication. Especially for newer faculty, it may help to allot time each week to work on writing projects. It is easy for new faculty to become overwhelmed with teaching and service activities. A permanent writing time each week will help to ensure that writing takes place on an ongoing basis. It also helps to identify the optimal place (i.e., office or home) to get the most uninterrupted quality writing time.

USING PREFERRED PROCESSES

Upon completion of the plan, the author implements each step with a continuous eye on the identified goals and criteria. The plan for production is useful as a guide toward achieving a writing goal. If a particular process is not working, the plan can be altered so long as the modifications are designed to achieve the goals and criteria previously set. One method for monitoring progress and quality is to design a matrix with the production steps on one axis and the quality criteria particular to that step on the other axis (see Table 11.1). By checking off work that has been completed, the author has the benefit of a graphic organizer that describes current progress and quality of work. Be sure to consider the purpose and goals, audience, and requirements relevant to particular journals as well as matters related to style and presubmission review. Aspects of each have been described earlier in this book.

EVALUATING PRODUCTS

When the manuscript is complete, it is important for the author to carefully review the work prior to submission for publication. The basis for the review is to:

- Evaluate the goals and purposes of the manuscript.
- Examine the criteria for achieving manuscript goals.
- Consider any additional criteria or considerations which emerged during production of the manuscript.

By practicing this form of evaluation, the author not only enhances the likelihood of achieving manuscript goals, but also reduces and even eliminates the likelihood of a rejection for publishers' technical reasons.

EVALUATING PROCESSES AND PROGRESS

Unless the author is disinclined to ever write again, it is particularly useful to review the processes for producing the manuscript. Such a review has two important benefits:

- Process review provides a reflective opportunity to consider the contribution of the completed manuscript to the broader goals and objectives of the writer. Questions can be addressed regarding the status in achieving the author's mission, the next steps toward achieving that purpose, and even the need for reconsideration of the strategies toward that end.
- Process review provides important insights to help the writer be effective in producing subsequent manuscripts. Address such

Table 11.1
Matrix for Monitoring Writing—Things to Consider

Area*	Effort				
Audience/Journal	Teachers/ Instructor	Teachers/ K–12 Education	Teachers/ Teacher Magazine	Teachers/ Kappan	Teachers/ Elementary School Journal
Style	Narrative Examples	Step-by-Step Examples	Essay Opinion	Descriptive with Data	APA Manual
Target Length	800 Words	1000 Words	5000 Words	2500 Words	No Limit
Submission Timeline		30 days	60 days	90 days	
Current Time Estimates	Hours @ 5 hours per week (one week buffer)				
Assigned Times	Monday-Friday 6:00–7:00 pm				
Required Examples	Need 3 (circle when completed)				
		1	2	3	
Pre-submission Review		Spelling	Punctuation	Grammar	
Audience Review		Pat Jones 2nd grade	Morgan Martin 5th grade	Sandy Ramone K–lst grade	

*Are goal and purpose clearly established? Prepare manuscript describing method for facilitating collaborative teaching in elementary school.

questions as, "What worked for me in producing this manuscript?" "What did not work effectively?" "What should I do differently next time?" "Where can I get support in the future if I need it?" Continuously monitoring professional progress will provide data to produce more effective production plans over time and to enhance overall writing success.

PERSPECTIVE

Professional development, including writing and scholarship, is a process that provides many opportunities for performance and continuous improvement. In the first chapter of this book, Obiakor, Algozzine, and Bakken noted that there are many reasons to write and all of them are important to professional educators: empowerment, free expression, being on cutting edge (fostering new knowledge), and pursuing intrinsic and extrinsic rewards. They also pointed out that there are many ways to approach writing and all of them are within the reach of all professional educators: Know your story and style, unmask yourself, talk less and write more, and collaborate more often.

Algozzine, Spooner, and Bauer, (Chapter 2) indicated that professional growth and development needs are among the central themes driving the writing interests of many educators. Integrating writing with other activities (e.g., teaching and service) improves the likelihood of success—this could be particularly intriguing for women and underrepresented groups in higher education. They offered the following suggestions to make the most of writing efforts: Identify a writing style that works for you; think of all writing as a work in progress; use technology to improve your productivity; set goals you can easily achieve; nothing breeds success like success; and build on your accomplishments, don't rest on them.

In Chapter 3, Obiakor, Ford, and Mutua presented additional reasons for writing. First, there are plenty of opportunities to create truths and respond to inaccuracies in the literature and, second, writing provides opportunities for self-determination within a career that are unavailable in other activities. Although their discussion centered on concerns of diverse, minority scholars, there are truths for all writers in what they have written: History is a good teacher, but it should not be a preemptor; opportunities for writing and improving written communication skills are everywhere, and negative attitudes do more to control productivity in negative people.

When considering challenges facing novice writers, Goor and Kolpin's (Chapter 4) message was clear: Fear of the unknown and competing priorities make scholarly productivity difficult to achieve. They suggest confronting them directly by finding passion, making writing time, pushing past writing blocks, cultivating creativity, dispelling myths, enlisting support, and editing ruthlessly provide positive guidance for becoming happily published.

Chapter 5 (Rueda and Monzó), Chapter 6 (Roth and Patton), and Chapter 7 (Mehring and Schwenn) illustrate very specific ways to enhance efforts to produce articles, books and other products, and proposals for submission to funding agencies. These activities are among expectations of university faculty and are the least likely content areas to be mastered in advanced graduate training programs.

To further assist progress from ideas to published products, Weaver (Chapter 8) illustrates the importance of technology and the many ways for writers to use it. Thurlow, Algozzine, Edyburn, and Obiakor (Chapter 9) and Edyburn, Spooner, Algozzine, and Obiakor (Chapter 10) add guidelines (e.g., using models to improve likelihood of success, and varying form and style with audience) for working with editors based on their own experiences serving on review boards of research-oriented and practice-oriented journals.

The contents of this book provide a strong foundation of guiding principles for professionals interested in writing. By implementing TQM principles, many authors will find answers to questions they have about professional development activities related to writing. Professionals engaging them find themselves less burdened with unfocused, unproductive writing activities. They also find they have more time to spend with other aspects of professional development (e.g., teaching and service).